Portrait of a Rebellion

English press reporting of the Easter Rising,
Dublin, Ireland, 1916

by
Dean Stiles

DEDICATION

To Sally, for inspiring me to study

CONTENTS

ACKNOWLEDGEMENTS

Special thanks to Professor David Welch and Dr Timothy
Bowman at the University of Kent School of History for their
help and guidance researching the master's dissertation on
which this book is based. Thanks also to the staff of the British
Library newspaper archive in Colindale.

.

.

FOREWORD

THIS WORK uses a representative sample of contemporary English newspapers to examine press reporting of the Easter Rising in Dublin, Ireland in 1916. It shows the extent to which the British government reacted to public opinion and attempted its influence by manipulating the flow of information to newspapers. Government efforts to play down the rising as unrepresentative of Irish constitutional nationalism were initially successful with its portrayal in newspapers as a German-orchestrated plot aided by a handful of radical extremists. However, government failure to manage the media impact in England of the subsequent military executions prompted powerful newspaper campaigns against the process that reignited interest and coverage of the rising. The opportunity for government to minimise the political repercussions of the rising in England and in Ireland was forfeit.

* * *

1 NEWSPAPERS AND PUBLIC OPINION

NEWSPAPERS are the primary source for this dissertation that examines English public opinion towards the Easter Rising, the particular positions English newspapers adopted towards the crisis, and how government responded to and managed newspaper coverage. The dissertation uses material selected from a representative sample of newspapers to make comparisons and connections between different newspapers and other sources to consider newspaper views within the wider sphere of political debate on Ireland and assess the extent to which government responded to, and attempted to manipulate, English public opinion during the period immediately following the rising.

Newspapers are a rich source for political historians of British and Irish history especially for that of the early decades of the 20th century when collectively newspapers were the largest single medium for communication.[1] Newspapers and periodicals were the principal means to shape and lead political debate and the best way to generate wider support

---

[1] *The Newspaper Press Directory 1916,* C Mitchell and Co Ltd (London 1916) lists 5,920 newspapers, periodicals, magazines and reviews published in 1916 including 160 morning and evening newspapers

among the electorate for particular political positions. They also show the links between politicians and journalists and reveal how information easily becomes propaganda when its source is concealed so that news becomes a form of instrumental knowledge designed to manipulate and control.[2] Newspapers are not a substitute for traditional sources on the basis that "the existing manuscript archives have been farmed to extinction" since the value of newspapers is dependent on their being read alongside traditional sources.[3] And, like these, newspapers pose a number of problems: how best to work with and select from a seemingly inexhaustible body of material and what this can reliably tell us about the past. The period covered by this dissertation – the start of the rising on Easter Monday, 24 April 1916, to Sir Roger Casement's execution on 3 August 1916 – limits the number of newspapers required for the sample to manageable proportions. Research was helped by using electronic archives, which are easier to store and access, that became available for *The Manchester Guardian, Observer,* and *The Daily Mirror* from spring 2008, in addition to *The Times* that has been accessible on-line at most libraries for some years. However, electronic search engines while useful cannot be relied upon to identify relevant material and do not obviate the need to trawl though a substantial body of material or, as is the case with the *Liverpool Echo,* to read original newspapers in such exceptionally frail condition that even turning pages is laborious and time consuming.

Newspapers provide much of the evidence for David George Boyce's study of British public opinion during the Irish War of Independence, published in 1972.[4] The originality of Boyce's approach lies in the

---

[2] John Mackenzie, 'The Press and the dominant ideology of empire' in Simon Potter, ed, *Newspapers and Empire in Ireland and Britain - Reporting the British Empire c1857-1921,* Four Courts Press (Dublin 2004) p26
[3] Alvin Jackson, review of D George Boyce and Alan O'Day, *The Ulster Crisis,* 1885-1921, ed, Palgrave Macmillan (London 2005) *English Historical Review* CXXIII: 492-495, 2008, pp 493-4
[4] D G Boyce, *Englishmen and Irish Troubles,* Jonathan Cape (London 1972)

sustained analysis of diverse sources that highlight the attention paid by government to British newspapers and other publications.[5] His premise is that during the late nineteenth and early twentieth centuries the press acted as a complement to other tools of political controversy. "The emphasis in this mode of historical writing is on the specifics: on identifiable individuals and groups seeking newspaper outlets for their opinions; on the detailed and sometimes closely reasoned political arguments and positions adopted by contemporaries; and, very often, on the close links that developed between the world of journalism and the world of politics. Such accounts stress the importance of debates conducted along largely rational lines, involving contingent and shifting attitudes and arguments that meshed with the minutiae of party politics."[6] Boyce's study stands out not only for its use of newspaper archives but also for "attempting to adjust the balance by investigating the period from a British rather than Irish standpoint".[7] Many of the themes he identifies, like British "boredom" with Irish constitutional issues unless overridden by some outside event, are evident during the Easter Rising.

More recently, a number of political histories using newspapers as primary sources have been published but most have an Irish focus. Michael Wheatley uses provincial papers to examine the period preceding the rising to show the declining fortunes of Irish nationalism against support for the Irish Parliamentary Party and Home Rule.[8] Marie-Louise Legg charts the rise of Irish nationalism in provincial newspapers from the 1850s and shows how these spread the ideas and methods of the Land League throughout

[5] Nicholas Mansergh, review of *Englishmen and Irish Troubles: British Public Opinion and the Making of Irish Policy*, 1918-1922, D G Boyce in *Political Science Quarterly*, Vol 89, No 3 (Autumn 1974) pp 699-700

[6] Simon J Potter, review of *The Eternal Paddy: Irish Identity and the British Press, 1798-1882* by Michael de Nie, Review no. 501) URL: http://www.history.ac.uk/reviews/ paper/ potter.html

[7] D G Boyce, *Englishmen and Irish Troubles*, Jonathan Cape (London 1972), pp13

[8] Michael Wheatley, *Nationalism and the Irish Party: Provisional Ireland 1910-1916*, Oxford University Press (Oxford 2005)

histories of events that have cultural significance, like the Easter Rising, there has been considerable reinterpretation of the event particularly in works by David Fitzpatrick, Charles Townsend and Tom Garvin.[14] Fitzpatrick explores the strictures and operation of participating organisations examining membership and motivation while Garvin places the rising in a much broader context of nationalist political behaviour. All three writers approach the period as one essentially of Irish nationalist movements in conflict with British rule with the Easter Rising one of a series of key events triggering change; the others being the 1918 election, the 1919-21 War of Independence, the 1921 Truce and Treaty, and the 1922 Civil War. Peter Hart challenges this narrative arguing that geographical distinctions can be as misleading as "periodisation and nomenclature" and suggests it is more useful to think of the Irish revolution as an ethnic power struggle rather than a national war of liberation.[15] Hart's "new revolutionary history" argues that the British government's failure to recognise the consequences of its actions suppressing the rising stemmed from the crudity of British thinking about Ireland, particularly within the military establishment. Undoubtedly racist and patronising attitudes prevailed among the land-owning Anglo Irish who constituted a disproportionate number of British army officers. However, by comparison with newspapers in the nineteenth century there is little overt expression of such stereotypical portrayals of the Irish in mainstream English newspapers during 1916 although implicit in almost all reporting is the unquestioning assumption of the merit and benefit of empire.

---

[14] David Fitzpatrick, *Politics and Irish Life 1913-1921, Provincial Experience of War and Revolution,* Cork University Press (Cork 1977) also *The Two Irelands 1912-1939,* Oxford University Press (Oxford 1998); Tom Garvin, *The Evolution of Irish Nationalist Politics,* Gill and Macmillan (Dublin 1981) also *Nationalist Revolutionaries in Ireland,* 1858-1928, Oxford University Press (Oxford 1987); Charles Townshend, *The British Campaign in Ireland 1891-1921,* Oxford University Press (London 1975), also *Political Violence in Ireland,* Clarendon Press (Oxford 1983) and *Easter 1916 - The Irish Rebellion,* Penguin Books (London 2006)
[15] Peter Hart, *The IRA at War 1916-1923,* Oxford University Press (Oxford 2003)

Critics of newspaper sources doubt if all the brouhaha in the many editorials, readers' letters, and often biased and misleading reporting had very much effect on the politics or the voting habits of a restricted electorate. Certainly recent studies that benefit from access to detailed opinion polling data suggest that newspapers, individually at least, have only limited influence on their readers' decision making.[16] However, it is not so much influence but the fact that newspapers provide an accurate guide to public attitudes on specific issues that is of interest. Britain's national newspapers and regional papers with large circulations operated during the period under discussion as an integral part of the established social order and so reflect a relatively narrow range of political and social opinion. The aim of most newspapers, especially those with large circulations driven by the need to sustain advertising revenues, was not primarily to lead public opinion, whatever their proprietors may have thought or desired, but to appeal to the interests, values and judgements of their target audience. However, in doing so newspapers would often anticipate shifts in public opinion and there is evidence of this in Wheatley's study that shows the change from majority support for Home Rule at the outbreak of war, to support for Irish nationalism following the rising, was not led by but rather reflected in provincial papers. When newspapers did try to lead on inappropriate issues circulation often fell, as happened to *The Daily Mirror* at the end of the war when its proprietor, Lord Rothermere, took a more active editorial role to campaign against his pet hates, a national health scheme and "squandermania" where he accused

---

[16] J Curtice, 'Was it the Sun wot won it again? The influence of newspapers in the 1997 election campaign, Centre for Research into Elections and Social Trends, Working Paper Number 75, Sept 1999. This study refutes the claim made by the *Sun* newspaper that its decision to support the Labour Party in the final weeks of the 1997 general election campaign was the decisive factor in the party's success. The study uses detailed opinion polling data to establish that no significant change in voting pattern among *Sun* readers occurred following its support for Labour

Lloyd George's government of frittering away the national's wealth.[17]

The sample of eight newspapers, five dailies, two Sundays and a regional paper used in this dissertation was based on national circulation as a measure of influence and taking into account political allegiance to ensure balance. A regional paper is also included to counter the national bias of the sample.[18] The newspapers studied are: the high circulation national dailies, *The Daily Mail, The Daily Mirror* and *The Daily News* with declared Unionist, independent and Liberal stances; The Unionist *Times*, and Liberal *Manchester Guardian*, with smaller, more elitist readerships but equally matched in terms of reputation and influence; two Sunday papers, the *Observer*, independent but usually taking a Unionist line, and the large circulation, Liberal supporting, *Lloyds Weekly News*. The *Liverpool Echo* represents regional papers, chosen specifically because of its large proportion of Irish origin readers.

The labels Unionist and Liberal are crude and do not reflect the subtlety of opinion in newspapers; in the case of *The Times* and *The Daily Mail*, this was dictated by those of their proprietor, Lord Northcliffe, who described his press as "Unionist and Imperialist" and "supporting the unwritten alliance of English speaking peoples".[19] *The Daily Mail* campaigned for causes like child poverty and social deprivation but by 1916 under Lord Rothermere's control had a distinctly less Liberal tone. The *Observer*, under J L Garvin's editorship, had a reputation for independence but generally propounded fluent and persuasive argument with a strong right wing bent.

---

[17] Bill Hagerty, *Read all about it! 100 sensational years of the Daily Mirror*, First Stone Publishing, (Lydney, Gloucestershire 2003) p28
[18] See appendix 3 for newspaper circulations and political allegiances
[19] J Lee Thompson, 'Fleet Street Colossus: The Rise and Fall of Northcliffe, 1896-1922' *Parliamentary History*, 2006, Vol 25 Issue 1, pp117

The Daily News, Thursday, 4 May 1916 The Daily News ran its first photographs showing scenes of devastation in Dublin post the rising in its 4 May 1916 issue. The Daily Mirror devoted the front page of the 11 May issue to the rebellion but with less dramatic pictures

2 THE RISING

THE EASTER RISING was one of few events that would overshadow war reporting in English newspapers for more than a week: it was "an astonishing piece of street theatre" with raging gun battles and house-to-house fighting in which 500 people died and 2,500 were wounded – the great majority civilians caught in the crossfire – and many more traumatised by the shocking events.[20] The suppression involved British artillery shelling the General Post Office and other buildings to create "an awesome Wagnerian inferno of smoke and flame" that shocked witnesses.[21] However, English readers would only read of this and it would be over a week before photographs appeared in papers and then showing only the aftermath, bad as it was, of the artillery shelling.[22] These images featured alongside equally dramatic photographs showing damage in Lowestoft following a German naval bombardment on the night of Tuesday April 25.[23]

---

[20] Keith Jeffery, *Ireland and the Great War*, Cambridge University Press (Cambridge 2000) p51
[21] Charles Townshend, *Easter 1916 – The Irish Rebellion*, Penguin Books (London 2006) p355
[22] *The Daily Mirror* published its first photographs showing scenes of devastation in Dublin post the rising in its 2 May 1916 issue and devoted the front page of the 11 May issue to the rebellion but with less dramatic pictures. *The Daily News* published its first photographs in 4 May and 5 May issues
[23] *The Daily News*, Thursday, 27 April 1916, p7

Even without the graphic imagery or eye witness accounts, news of the rising was sufficiently shocking to lead, and sometimes fill entirely, the news pages of all English newspapers. These were scenes to match the devastation described and pictured by English newspapers of the Western Front but made more dramatic because the attack was from inside the empire when the country was "in the throes of a great war" during "the great conflict for the liberties of all and the future of a pacific civilization."[24]

The rising had added shock value for English audiences because it came after an eighteen-month lull in coverage by newspapers of Irish issues. The priority that Ireland had for English politicians, and with it the extensive coverage of Irish affairs in English newspapers that resulted from parliamentary debates on Home Rule, ended in August 1914. Ireland, from an English perspective, was subordinate to the war effort and low in the order of government priorities determined by the strategic demands of a conflict that even in 1914 politicians realised would be considerable. Herbert Asquith, the Liberal prime minister, put Irish matters on the long finger: he struck a deal with Sir Edward Carson, the Irish Unionist leader and with Andrew Bonar Law, the Conservative leader, to withdraw their opposition to the Home Rule Bill. This was conditional on the bill remaining suspended until the end of hostilities – few at the time expected this to be more than months away – and with a guarantee of some as yet unspecified provision for special treatment of Ulster.[25] The act providing Home Rule received Royal Assent in 18 September to make Ireland, so long a source of bitter debate, "the one bright spot" on the map of Europe.[26] For English newspaper readers, preoccupied with the war, the Irish Question had been settled, a view helped by support for the war effort from

---

[24] *Manchester Guardian*, Wednesday, 26 April 1916, p4
[25] Charles Townshend, *Easter 1916 – The Irish Rebellion*, Penguin Books (London 2006) p61
[26] Foreign secretary, Sir Edward Grey, speaking in parliament, Hansard, LXV, col. I829, 3 Aug 1914

constitutional nationalists in the Irish Parliamentary Party and from
Unionists who realised such help would establish their patriotic credentials
when the home rule struggle renewed at the end of hostilities. In Ireland,
Britain and across the Empire a patriotic surge manifest itself in high levels
of volunteering for military service in the British army and a thirst for news
of the war. Newspaper circulation and recruitment follow a similar pattern
with initial surges from August 1914 before suffering sharp declines from
mid-1915.[27] Statistics, whether for newspaper circulation or recruitment
are treacherous, and none more so than those for newspapers from this
period, but there is a degree of reliability to *The Daily Mail*'s circulation
claims that illustrate the overall trend.[28] *The Daily Mail* recorded its highest
daily wartime sales of 1.227 million on 15 May 1915, shortly after the
passenger liner Lusitania was torpedoed and sunk, after which sales fell
steadily for the duration of the war.[29] The fall in newspaper circulation
reflects disillusion with the war and lack of military success. By the spring
of 1916 war news was bleak despite the best efforts of government, military
and complicit newspaper reporters to spin otherwise; the Allied offensive
the previous autumn had failed to break the stalemate on the Western
Front, by January the Gallipoli campaign had ended in defeat, and in late
January the Military Service Act introduced conscription to the mainland.
The steadily mounting casualty and death rate saw obituaries with
accompanying postage stamp size portraits of young officers begin to
proliferate in even the large circulation dailies and the Easter Rising would

---

[27] Charles Townshend, *Easter 1916 – The Irish Rebellion,* Penguin Books (London 2006) pp 64-
65
[28] *The Daily Mail*'s circulation is based on published, independently audited statements
showing daily sales issued as part of its circulation war with its main rival *The Daily Mirror*
[29] *The Daily Mail*, 5 July 1915. It was not until 1921 that it again reached these 1915 peaks.
See Appendix 3 for other circulation changes

add its share.[30] This was the backdrop against which Ireland, after an eighteen-month absence, appeared in English newspapers but unlike pre-war coverage when news was determined by parliamentary reporting, in 1916 it was shocking events within Ireland that dominated news pages. For the first time, war reporting, even of events as dramatic as the surrender of General Townsend and his forces at Kut on 29 April 1916, was placed down-page.[31]

The opening moments of the Easter Rising went unreported, subsumed by the gravity of the rising itself. It started at noon on Easter Monday when Constable O'Brien, on duty at the main gate of Dublin Castle, was shot during an abortive attack on the Castle. Major Ivor Price, the British Intelligence Officer in Ireland, who was in the Castle attending a meeting with Sir Matthew Nathan, under secretary of State for Ireland, immediately concluded that a rebel attack was taking place. By 12.15pm Price had alerted the military headquarters in Phoenix Park by telephone and Nathan had informed the Chief Secretary for Ireland, Augustine Birrell who was in London, by telegram.[32] And about an hour after this, the military authorities in Ireland provided details of its response to the situation to London in a message sent by naval wireless.[33] The government delayed announcing the news until the following evening taking advantage of the loss of the telegraphic service at 12.20pm when the rebels cut the telegraph

---

[30] *Lloyds Weekly News*, 7 May 1916, p7, was unusual in publishing similar style obituaries with portraits of Pearse and MacDonagh, who were executed, and O'Rahilly, who was shot as he left the GPO during the rebellion

[31] General Townsend had struggled through a 143-day siege at Kut, an obscure town in Mesopotamia until compelled to surrender in the face of overwhelming Turkish forces on 29 April. His surrender was a blow to British prestige, comparable with the fall of Singapore in 1942, and all the daily papers carried detailed reports the following day. The detail contained in the Press Bureau announcement and its speed contrasts with the delay and brevity of its first statements reporting the rising

[32] Michael Foy and Brian Barton, *The Easter Rising*, Sutton Publishing (Stroud 1999) p84

[33] Despatch from Field Marshal Sir John French, Commanding in Chief, Home Forces. Printed in the Supplement to the London Gazette of 21 July 1916: www.gazettes-online.co.uk

connection. However, the telephone system remained operational throughout the rising, contrary to the first government statement, and was under military control from 5pm on Monday at which point civilians could only receive, not initiate calls.[34] News of the rising became public in England with a government statement, made by Birrell on Tuesday evening to the House of Commons, stating that "a large body of men identified with the Sinn Feiners, mostly armed, occupied St Stephen's Green and took possession forcibly of the Post Office, where they cut the telegraphic and telephonic wires."[35]

---

[34] Michael Foy and Brian Barton, *The Easter Rising*, Sutton Publishing (Stroud 1999) p297
[35] The Press Bureau statement is shown in appendix 4

3 SINN FÉIN TAKES THE BLAME

THE DELAYED Press Bureau statement and the paucity of information made available significantly altered the way the story was presented by all newspapers. The lack of any detailed information for either story encouraged newspapers to speculate and portray the rising as part of a German plot to subvert England. Tuesday's editions led with news of the arrest of Sir Roger Casement in Ireland and the attempting to smuggle arms into the country on board a German ship. This was immediately linked in the following day's editions to the news of the Easter Rising and gave Casement a much higher profile in coverage of the rising than his marginal role warranted. Casement had a high public profile in England, initially with favourable press coverage of his role in exposing the Putumayo atrocities in South America for which he was knighted in 1911. The atrocity scandal became public in 1912 and Casement appeared before the Commons Select Committee investigating the affair in London the following year, which also received extensive publicity. However, even at this stage newspapers saw him as an exotic figure, "a speaker of fame" who "combined citizenship of the world with an enthusiastic attachment to

3 SINN FÉIN TAKES THE BLAME

**Press Bureau statement announcing the rising
25 April 1916**

The following announcement has been received from the Chief Secretary for Ireland:

At noon yesterday serious disturbances broke out in Dublin.

• A large body of men identified with the Sinn Feiners, mostly armed, occupied Stephen's Green and took possession forcibly of the Post Office, where they cut the telegraphic and telephonic wires.

• Houses were also occupied in Stephen's Green, Sackville Street, Abbey Street and along the quays.

• In the course of the day soldiers arrived from the Curragh, and the situation is now, well in hand.

• So far as is known here three military officers, four or five soldiers, two loyal volunteers and two policemen have been killed, and four or five military officers, seven or eight soldiers and six loyal volunteers wounded.

• No exact information has been received of casualties on the side of the Sinn Feiners.

• Reports received from Cork, Limerick, Ennis, Tralee and both Ridings of Tipperary show that no disturbances of any kind have occurred in these localities.

Press Bureau, Tuesday, 8.15 pm

romantic Nationalism".[36] But by 1914, his call for "a rifle for every Irish nationalist" saw a far less favourable portrayal in newspapers.[37] Newspaper tolerance evaporated when Casement appeared in Germany and publicly called, in an open letter published in the *Irish Independent* on 17 September 1914, for Irishmen not to serve in the British army. And by October 1915, a year after Casement's arrival in Germany *The Times* is quoting reports from the *Catholic Herald* detailing "the fullest evidence yet available of the German plot to enrol Irish prisoners of war in Germany in an Irish Brigade."[38] A letter to the editor in *The Times*, that called on the Foreign Office to withdraw Casement's consular pension granted in August, probably caught the public mood. The foreign secretary, Sir Edward Grey, received the same request, curiously using almost identical wording to the letter, in a Commons question a few months later.[39] The headline story of Casement's arrest was based on a short Admiralty statement issued by the Press Bureau on Monday stating that on the previous Thursday evening or Friday morning a German auxiliary vessel, disguised as a neutral merchant ship, had sunk while attempting to land arms and ammunition in Ireland and that Casement had been taken prisoner. It was, said the *Liverpool Echo*, in an unintentionally perspicacious comment made in a two-column lead story, "one of the most sensational incidents of the war" and it marked the start of almost two weeks of intensive news coverage by English national and regional papers of events in Ireland.[40] Press judgement on Casement was instant: "British capture the traitor Sir R. Casement".[41] With little new information other than the Admiralty statement newspapers were obliged to repeat much of what was already known about Casement

---

[36] *The Times*, 25 October 1913, p9
[37] *The Times*, 1 May 1914, p8
[38] *The Times*, 27 October 1915, p7
[39] *The Times*, 5 February 1915, p10
[40] *Liverpool Echo*, Tuesday, 25 April 1916
[41] *The Daily Mirror*, Tuesday, 25 April 1916, p3

including details of his consular service, knighthood and support for Irish nationalism.

Wednesday's front pages, breaking the news of the rising in Dublin, upstaged news of Casement's capture and the attempted landing of arms but the stories were immediately linked in order to pad out the sparse details available. Portraying the rising as a German-inspired plot and part of a larger plan tapped into a long-held view that Ireland was the "Achilles Heel of the empire, a source of comfort and indeed strength to England's enemies in time of war."[42] This also increased English reader interest in what was essentially a foreign, even if colonial, story. Newspapers had also to bring English readers up to speed on less well-known aspects of Irish nationalism, particularly Sinn Féin. Under its banner headline "Armed Sinn Feiners attempt to seize Dublin", *The Daily Mail* explained that Sinn Feiners[43] are "Irish malcontents" and that Sinn Féin means "All for Ourselves".[44] It is an inaccurate rendering of the Irish, perhaps innocently made but nonetheless an ingenious misinterpretation of "Ourselves Alone" or "We Ourselves" which lacks the hint of anti-Britishness the *Mail* introduced. The *Liverpool Echo,* in an explanatory note to its news, said more accurately that "roughly 'Sinn Fein' means 'ourselves' and Sinn Feiners are 'all for Ireland' without any qualification". Wednesday's national newspaper accounts, based on Birrell's statement, contain little additional information other than that issued by the Press Bureau and

---

[42] David G Boyce, 'British Opinion, Ireland, and the War, 1916-1918' *The Historical Journal,* Vol 17, No 3 (Sep 1974) pp 575-593. This argument was powerfully made by S Rosenbaum (ed) *Against Home Rule - the Case for the Union* (London, 1912), especially pp 11-12, and the essays contributed by Admiral Lord Charles Beresford on ' Home Rule and Naval Defence', pp 189-94, and by the Earl Percy on 'The military disadvantages of Home Rule', pp 195-203. These views resurfaced briefly in early coverage of the rising by Unionist papers
[43] English newspapers almost universally adopted the hybrid Irish-English word Sinn Feiners, spelt without the accent
[44] *The Daily Mirror,* Wednesday, 26 April 1916, front page

THE DAILY MIRROR. Wednesday, April 26, 1916.

REBEL ATTEMPT TO CAPTURE DUBLIN.—Official

The Daily Mirror

CERTIFIED CIRCULATION LARGER THAN THAT OF ANY OTHER DAILY PICTURE PAPER

No. 3,902.   Registered at the G.P.O. as a Newspaper.   WEDNESDAY, APRIL 26, 1916   One Halfpenny.

ATTEMPTED RISING IN DUBLIN: MR. BIRRELL'S STATEMENT IN THE HOUSE OF COMMONS YESTERDAY.

The Post Office, Dublin.

Mr. Birrell arriving at the House yesterday.

Sir Roger Casement.

Lord Wimborne, Ireland's Lord-Lieutenant.

Following upon the capture of the renegade Sir Roger Casement and the sinking of a German warship that was carrying arms and ammunition to Ireland comes the news that there has been a serious rising in the Irish capital itself. Mr. Birrell, the Chief Secre-tary for Ireland, announced yesterday in the House of Commons that the Dublin rioters had seized the Post Office and were in possession of some portions of the city itself. Twelve lives were lost during the riot.

The Daily Mirror, Wednesday, 26 April 1916
Wednesday's front pages, breaking the news of the rising in Dublin, upstaged news of Casement's capture and the attempted landing of arms but the stories were immediately linked in order to pad out the sparse details available

almost all identify Sinn Féin with the rebellion and implicitly portray Sinn Féin as a formidable, structured, organisation. Newspapers continue to identify the rebels as Sinn Féin in their coverage with the exception of *Lloyds Weekly News*,[45] which preferred "rebels" and a "rebellion" matching similar language of Press Bureau statements. Sinn Féin was a useful catchall label for newspapers and, given the paucity of information in the first statement, a reflection also of how little government knew of who was behind the rising.

Sinn Féin emerged in 1905 from Cumann na nGaedheal, a loose political ginger group set up by Arthur Griffith five years before. It was revolutionary in the sense that its aim was to subvert British rule but the method was non-violent, advocating a form of passive resistance by ignoring British rule. It was a new approach to the idea of Irish independence and one that included cultural, hence the use of the Gaelic name, as well as economic and political development. A variety of people coalesced around Griffith who was less the leader and more of an inspirational figure for the movement. It was also a useful front for the highly secretive Irish Republican Brotherhood, of which Griffith was a member, and used by it as a vehicle for publishing pamphlets and other material. Griffith's newspaper, *Sinn Féin,* set up in 1906 was shut down by the authorities in November 1914, as well as its short-lived successors, *Eire-Ireland, Scissors and Paste,* and the *Nationalist* which appeared in 1915. But Griffith's extensive writing meant that Sinn Féin, despite its relative obscurity in political terms, was well known even in England unlike the groups that organised the rising. Birrell's identification of Sinn Féin with the rebels made in the Press Bureau statement has its origins in September 1914 when British authorities in Ireland chose to identify Eoin MacNeill's

---

[45] In 1916 *Lloyds Weekly News* was Britain's second highest circulation Sunday newspaper after the *News of the World*

breakaway Irish Volunteers group as "Sinn Fein Volunteers". There does not seem to be any reason for this as Sinn Féin was never associated with the Volunteers or MacNeil identified with Sinn Féin.[46] But in 1916 Sinn Féin was an extremely effective label that encouraged newspapers to identify the rising with a handful of known extremists and government clearly briefed newspapers about this since they repeat the erroneous link. Before Birrell's statement to the Commons, the *Liverpool Echo,* in its Tuesday edition with news of Casement's arrest, incorrectly details Casement's connection with Sinn Féin, described as a political party formed from a breakaway section of the National Volunteers that claimed allegiance to Casement. *The Observer* is the only paper in the sample to provide detailed and accurate analysis of Sinn Féin. In a harsh critique of its philosophy, the paper noted that there "was an increasing lack of common sense until the movement became a mere refurbishing of Feinism". *The Observer* challenged Sinn Féin's ideas on economic independence of Britain and the Sinn Féin cultural agenda: "The Irish were not only to talk their original language officially – how that was to help in the solution of the Ulster question nobody knew – but were to have their own manufactures. Protection against British goods was somehow to be combined with free exportation of Irish products into British markets, and the best was to be made of both worlds."[47] But such detailed analysis was unusual and for most papers Sinn Féin supporters were "either avowedly pro-German" or are at least opposed to recruiting in Ireland and committed to the "monstrous doctrine" that Ireland should remain neutral in the war.[48]

The English press universally condemned the instigators of the rebellion. "The deeds of the Huns in Belgium and elsewhere were nothing

---

[46] Charles Townshend, *Easter 1916 – The Irish Rebellion,* Penguin Books (London 2006) p80
[47] *Observer,* Sunday 30 April 1916, p8
[48] *The Manchester Guardian,* Wednesday, 26 April 1916, p5

to the Sinn Fein fanatics. They were in the crazy mood to welcome hell itself if the devil and his legions would only come forth against the British flag."[49] The rising was characterised as "the wild act of a small and violent faction"[50] but there was no denunciation of Irish Nationalists as a whole. Most newspapers portrayed the event as an insult and a blow to Ireland as much as it was to England; it seemed "to be the fate of Ireland to act as a lodestone to the enemies of this kingdom".[51] The rising cast "a wholly underserved slur on the loyalty, patriotism, and good sense of that great majority of the Irish people against whom much more than anyone else the movement is directed."[52] The *Liverpool Echo,* matching national papers in terms of its coverage of the rising and opinion about it, commented that "there are other Home Rulers in Ireland besides the nationalists, namely the small but aggressive Sinn Fein party" but "if few [Nationalists] were republicans, fewer still desired a German victory."[53] Newspapers implicitly recognised the danger the rising posed for constitutional nationalists. *The Observer,* not a natural supporter of the leader of the Irish Parliamentary Party, John Redmond, rallied to his defence and brought an international dimension: "With Mr Redmond there is profound and universal sympathy in this country. He has had to contend with indescribable difficulties, and his moral influence not only in Ireland but, above all, in the United States, has been almost priceless to the Empire."[54]

Newspapers were reluctant to let the "new anxiety" the rising posed reopen the Home Rule debate on the basis that it was "unreasonable to make capital against Home Rule out of this criminal insurrection of the Sinn

---

[49] *Observer,* Sunday, 30 April 1916, p8
[50] *The Manchester Guardian,* Wednesday, 26 April 1916, p4
[51] *The Morning Post* quoted in David G Boyce, 'British Opinion, Ireland, and the War, 1916-1918' *The Historical Journal,* Vol 17, No 3 (Sep 1974) p576
[52] *The Manchester Guardian,* Wednesday, 26 April 1916, p4
[53] *Liverpool Echo,* Wednesday, 26 April 1916, news page without folio
[54] *Observer,* Sunday, 30 April 1916, p8

Feiners".[55] But it was not unreasonable to make capital against the government and in the week that followed the rising newspapers universally blamed government inaction in Ireland as its cause and newspaper political allegiances quickly surfaced. Asquith was already suffering a relentless public campaign against his government's handling of the war from Lord Northcliffe through his papers, *The Times* and *The Daily Mail*. Asquith's decision to form a coalition government in May 1915 and bring Unionists into the cabinet was motivated in part to moderate attacks from Unionist newspapers but had not entirely succeeded in this respect. *The Daily Mail* and *The Times* seized on the rising and were quick to exploit the crisis as "the natural result of the Government's policy in Ireland".[56] Asquith's government, but most especially the Irish administration and the Chief Secretary for Ireland, came under fierce criticism from newspapers, including Liberal supporting papers, for allowing the militarization of Irish politics with the formation of rival political armies: the Ulster Volunteer Force loyal to Irish Unionist MP Sir Edward Carson in 1913 and the National Volunteers created in response to this perceived Unionist threat and loosely under the control of Redmond from late 1913. Newspapers implicitly blamed these two armies for the rising, apart from the *Observer*, which is the only paper to acknowledge in any detail the role of the Irish Citizen Army led by James Connolly.[57] This was created as a workers' defence force following the dock strike and Dublin lockout of 1913, and provided the mainstay of the rebels along with Ireland's fourth political army, the Irish Volunteers. This splinter group, led by Eoin MacNeill, broke from the National Volunteers in September 1914

---

[55] *The Daily Telegraph* quoted in David G Boyce, 'British Opinion, Ireland, and the War, 1916-1918' *The Historical Journal*, Vol 17, No 3 (Sep 1974) p576
[56] *The Daily Mail*, Wednesday, 6 April 1916, p5
[57] *The Observer*, Sunday, 30 April 1916, p8

and was largely controlled by the secretive Irish Republican Brotherhood.[58] *The Daily News and Leader* labelled the government's failure to deal firmly with Carson's UVF "a fatal abdication of authority" that "gave a sanction to the spirit of lawlessness" which inspired the rebels.[59] *The Daily Mail* laid the blame with Asquith through Birrell's failure to deal with the Irish Volunteers: Asquith and Birrell "sat still and allowed a rebel force to be enrolled and armed... The Irish Volunteers paraded 1000 strong on College Green, most of them armed with rifles.... No one stopped them or challenged them, Mr Birrell never asked for what purpose the Volunteers existed. He knew that it was not to serve against the enemy, but rather to obstruct the Imperial forces."[60] The rising was a heaven sent opportunity for Unionist papers like *The Times* and *The Daily Mail* to discredit Birrell and thus Asquith's government. *The Times* maintained its attacks on Birrell for his "failure to maintain respect for law and order during the nine years of his weak and callous administration" and called for the government to "enforce measures to overawe sedition and suppress Sinn Fein".[61] *The Times* and *The Daily Mail* pursued their attacks on Asquith's government to the extent that their coverage of the Easter Rising was less to inform readers than discredit the government. While *The Times* had the nationalist Irish Volunteers in mind when it criticised Birrell for his weak administration, *The Manchester Guardian* recognised that from a German perspective, it was "the rebellion of Ulster, indeed, to which she [Germany] primarily looked".[62] Newspaper coverage split along political lines but within this there are more subtle differences: Unionist papers like *The Times* and *The Daily Mail* took a very English-centric view using the rising to highlight the

---

[58] Charles Townshend, *Political Violence in Ireland,* Clarendon Press (Oxford 1983) p261
[59] *The Daily News and Leader,* Monday, 1 May 1916, p4
[60] *The Daily Mail,* Wednesday, 26 April 1916, p4
[61] *The Times,* Wednesday, 26 April 1916, p7
[62] *The Manchester Guardian,* Wednesday 26 April, 1916 p4

failure of government policy on Ireland, while Liberal supporting papers like *The Manchester Guardian, The Daily News* and *Lloyds Weekly News,* all advocates of Home Rule, gave a much higher priority to the implications of the rising for Ireland. *The Manchester Guardian* hoped that "the moral of this lamentable affair will be rightly read and acted upon" but stressed that the "only people who can effectively maintain order, without violence or bloodshed, in Ireland are the Irish themselves."[63]

---

[63] *The Manchester Guardian,* Wednesday 26 April, 1916 p4

4 CENSORSHIP

THERE WAS unanimous opposition from newspapers towards the extent of censorship exercised by government over the Irish crisis. This was despite their willing participation in the censorship system where the government issued periodical notices to editors giving specific advice on the treatment of particular information.[64] The system had legal sanction under the Defence of the Realm Act but newspapers were also alarmed by new attempts to stop press comment that arose when both Houses of Parliament sat in secret session on Tuesday 25 April with an order in council that made it an offence for newspapers to report any reference of the proceeds at cabinet meetings. This was essentially an attempt to stop cabinet ministers privately briefing newspapers. *The Daily Mail* launched a ferocious attack on "putting the press out of action" by smuggling through "under cover of an entirely inappropriate occasion, a dramatic new set of rules which are capable of preventing discussion of the affairs of any public office."[65] *The*

---

[64] These D-notices covered every aspect of the war effort including air raids, food shortages, and shipping losses. A list of some fifty editors to whom confidential information could be relayed was maintained by the Press Bureau that was set up on 7 August 1914 to operate the censorship system

[65] *The Daily Mail*, Tuesday, 25 April 1916, p7

Ireland.[9] Several of the contributions in the work edited by D George Boyce and Alan O'Day draw on newspaper archives.[10] The more broad-based study of the British Empire, edited by Simon J Potter, examines newspapers and periodicals as devices that shaped the attitudes of the English, Welsh, Scots and Irish towards the British Empire and explores the relationship between the press, government and commercial interests.[11]

The focus of this dissertation is specifically with the British government's reaction to the Easter Rising and the extent to which English public opinion, derived in the main from newspapers, influenced government decision making when handling the crisis in April and May 1916. Charles Townshend's recent work is of direct relevance to this dissertation and the British perspective is one of several themes he explores. His assessment of the reaction of the British government and British army to the growth of Irish nationalism and his discussion of the transformation of opinion on all sides is one of the highlights of the book.[12] He limits discussion of the rebellion mainly to events in Dublin, arguing that the provincial rising hardly amounted to an emergency. Although some reviewers have criticised the book for this Dublin focus, it reflects that of English newspaper reporting which barely mentioned incidents outside Dublin except in very general terms.[13] Townshend's book, published to coincide with the 90th anniversary of the rising, includes the results of his research using accounts by participants in the Easter Rebellion assembled by the Bureau of Military History but released only in 2003. As with all

[9] Marie-Louise Legg, *Newspapers and Nationalism: the Irish provincial press, 1850-1892*, Four Courts Press, (Dublin1999)
[10] D George Boyce and Alan O'Day, eds, *The Ulster Crisis, 1885 - 1921*, Palgrave Macmillan (London 2005)
[11] Simon J Potter, ed, *Newspapers and Empire in Ireland and Britain - Reporting the British Empire c1857-1921*, Four Courts Press (Dublin 2004)
[12] Charles Townshend, *Easter 1916 - The Irish Rebellion*, Penguin Books (London 2006)
[13] Alan O'Day Review: Charles Townshend, *Easter 1916 - The Irish Rebellion*, Penguin Books (London 2006) *English Historical Review* CXXII: 849-850, 2007

Daily Mail in its leader on Wednesday accused the government of a "hide-
the-truth" policy, a play on its earlier and long running "Wait and Lose"
campaign against the government.[66] Before the war, *The Daily Mail*'s
proprietor, Lord Northcliffe had advocated "absolute, or prolonged
detention, of publication of telegraphic war news" and thought
governments "lacked understanding of the effect of the modern newspaper"
but when war came he showed no inclination to support such measures
and was one of the government's foremost critics through his newspapers.[67]
As a measure of government concern over adverse press comment, the first
meetings of Asquith's coalition cabinet in 1915 considered the question of
suppressing newspapers by executive action without the need for previous
prosecutions of newspapers. Government power over newspapers was
formidable and although exercised frequently in Ireland and England it was
mainly against small circulation newspapers, usually holding radical
opinions, and rarely against national papers, partly because they were too
useful and partly because their owners and editors were influential
members of the polity who often received information to support their
criticism of the government directly from cabinet ministers and
commanders in the field.[68]

After Birrell's first statement on Tuesday afternoon, and a short
narrative of events given by Lord Lansdowne on the Thursday advising that
the City Hall and the Four Courts were among the buildings occupied by

[66] *The Daily Mail*, Wednesday, 26 April 1916, p9
[67] Barry McGill, 'Asquith's Predicament, 1914-1918' *The Journal of Modern History*, Vol 39
No 3 (Sept 1967) p288
[68] The Shell Crisis of 1915 was exposed in an article in *The Times* on 14 May 1915 written by
its war correspondent, Colonel Charles à Court Repington, claiming that the Battle of Neuve
Chapelle failed due to a lack of shells and was based on information provided to *The Times* by
the Commander-in-Chief, Field Marshal Sir John French. Lloyd George, chancellor,
encouraged Northcliffe to publish the story in *The Times* and *Daily Mail* in a bid to unseat Lord
Kitchener who had responsibility for munitions production opinion. Cited in John M McEwen,
'Northcliffe and Lloyd George at War, 1914-1918', *The Historical Journal*, Vol 24, No 3 (Sept
1981) p655

"Sinn Feiners", newspapers had to wait until Friday before the government released detailed information about the rising. By this stage the delay in issuing press briefings was not because of lack of government information, undoubtedly an issue on Tuesday. Nathan had briefed the cabinet and by Thursday it was clear that the military had a firm grip on the situation with all Dublin's strategic points, including the harbour, secure, and outlying rebel points like those near the castle, captured, and the rebel headquarters in the GPO isolated from the remaining rebel strongholds. The cabinet was aware that the rebellion had been contained and there was no evidence of it spreading across Ireland. Nonetheless, it was only on Friday that government felt sufficiently confident to issue a detailed press statement that formed the basis for much of the reporting in Saturday's issues. *The Manchester Guardian,* like all nationals, showed its willingness to comply with censorship and revealed that it knew of the outbreak at five o'clock on Tuesday morning but was unable to publish information "in advance of an official announcement".[69] Government censorship undoubtedly antagonised the press, even those usually inclined to offer support, encouraging the hostile treatment it received. The brevity of government statements and obfuscation in the language used to describe events, like Birrell's assurance that "the situation was well in hand" on the Tuesday, plus the fact that government was the sole source of what little information was available on everything connected with the rising, raised newspaper suspicions. *The Time*s quoted Birrell's statement to contrast "grave disturbances" with his assurance that the situation was "well in hand" and queried inconsistencies in the government statement on communications, particularly Birrell's excuse about lack of telegraphic communication. It also queried the Admiralty statement, about the seizure of the German

---

[69] *The Manchester Guardian*, Wednesday 26 April 26, 1916 p4

29

auxiliary, which was extremely vague about the timing of events and failed to name the landing site.[70] The dearth of information led to much speculation and many false assumptions grossly inflating German involvement in the rising. "They (Germans] have striven to provoke it from the outbreak of the war, and at last they have succeeded in getting their dupes to indulge in an insane rising", said *The Times* claiming, "It is evidently the result of a carefully arranged plot, concocted between the Irish traitors and their German confederates." All the papers drew identical conclusions that the timing of the Zeppelin attack the previous Monday and the raid by a German navy cruiser squadron on Lowestoft on Wednesday were co-ordinated events. "The whole series of assaults were pretty obviously related, and were intended to support each other, and by their combined and cumulative effect to produce the deeper impression of terror here, of exultation in Germany."[71] Such conclusions are understandable given the fevered atmosphere of wartime England but that all newspapers should independently arrive at them and express them in similar language seems too coincidental and points to more systematic private briefings by ministers and officials. That this view so suited the government wishing to deflect criticism from its Irish policies reinforces the premise.

Newspapers speculated about plots and rumours, although the latter had more foundation, but also reminded readers of the constraints limiting newspaper reporting. *The Daily Mirror*[72] alluded on the Tuesday, before newspapers published reports of the rising, to unsubstantiated information of "some plot in which Casement was concerned". On the rising, *The Daily Mail's* leader found "it difficult to believe that if newspapers has been permitted to publish the information which was in their hands on Sunday

[70] *The Times*, Wednesday 26 April 1916, p7
[71] *The Manchester Guardian*, Wednesday, 26 April 1916, p4
[72] *The Daily Mirror*, Tuesday, 25 April 1916, p3

night these events could have happened". The "information" would also have included the Volunteers manifesto, published by the Dublin based, and Unionist, *Evening Mail* as part of a campaign by the Cork landowner, Unionist peer, and former secretary of state for war, Lord Midleton, to get Birrell and Nathan to take decisive action against the Volunteers. [73] Midleton had demanded, unsuccessfully, that Birrell allow the publication of the manifesto in "the better class of newspaper" so that the public should know, as he saw it, the truth of this "subversive" movement".[74] However, newspapers were also aware of reports circulating a day before the rising in New York among Clan-na-Gael members, the United States-based Irish nationalist organisation with which Casement had contact during his visit in 1914, that a "'serious revolution' had broken out in Dublin and supposedly had met with a considerable amount of success."[75] The *Liverpool Echo*, in its Tuesday edition before news of the rising was public, had linked the Casement story with a smaller item detailing an "outrage" when shots were fired at police attempting to remove a telegraph pole knocked down to stop an excursion train on Ireland's Great Southern and Western Railway. *The Echo* credited *The Daily Telegraph* and *The Star*'s Dublin correspondent for the story: it was commonplace at this time to publish stories from other newspapers, especially when information was scarce as was the case during the Easter Rising.[76] In normal circumstances, English papers would have relied on Dublin papers for detailed information but these were seriously disrupted; *The Express* offices were occupied by Volunteers after the abortive Castle attack and the offices of the *Freeman's Journal,* near the GPO, were destroyed by fire early in the week. Only the Unionist *Irish*

---

[73] *Evening Mail*, Monday, 27 March 1916

[74] Charles Townshend, *Easter 1916 – The Irish Rebellion,* Penguin Books (London 2006) p144

[75] *The Times* New York correspondent, in a report dated 25 April in *The Times,* 29 April 1916, p10

[76] These stories are in addition to the reports from the western front supplied by a small syndicate of reporters approved by the military as part of wartime press censorship

Times managed a few editions at the beginning of the week. The railway outrage story, one of only a few that week with an acknowledged Dublin correspondent as a source, was about a minor incident in Ireland but received unusually wide coverage in English national newspapers, including *The Manchester Guardian* not prone to running relatively lightweight stories of this nature.[77] Newspapers were aware of reports that troubles were likely over Easter. *The Manchester Guardian* found it "somewhat inexplicable" that the Irish Executive had failed to keep a sufficient force immediately available in Dublin "to suppress at once a movement which might have been foreseen and which had, indeed, been a subject of rumour and speculation before it took place".[78] This knowledge increased newspaper suspicion and doubts about the government's portrayal of the true extent of the crisis but none was willing to challenge restrictions on publication. However, *The Manchester Guardian*, did recall that at a meeting of the Dublin Corporation, the week before the rising, one of the members read a memorandum which purported to have been drawn up by Dublin Castle authorities instructing the police and military to hold various points of vantage in the city in the event of a rising. The paper dryly noted, "This memorandum was officially declared at the time to be a fabrication."[79] However, Townshend suggests that the document was genuine but not, as thought at the time, a plan for immediate action. "It was despatched from Major General Sir Lovick Friend, General Officer Commanding in Ireland, to the Irish Office in London detailing precautionary measures in the event of conscription being imposed."[80]

The *Observer* criticised government inaction when it and the press was aware that "grave mischief was afoot" in Ireland but when cabinet

---

[77] *The Manchester Guardian*, Wednesday, 26 April 1916, p5
[78] *The Manchester Guardian*, Wednesday, 26 April 1916, p4
[79] *The Manchester Guardian*, Wednesday, 26 April 1916, p5
[80] Charles Townshend, *Easter 1916 – The Irish Rebellion*, Penguin Books (London 2006) p133

members "were thinking much more of muffling the Press than putting down the Sinn Fein."[81] *The Manchester Guardian* was equally sceptical about the Press Bureau statements noting: "We are permitted only to receive the most meagre reports of what is happening in Ireland, but we are told that soldiers who ought never to have left Dublin have been recalled and that military authorities have the situation 'well in hand,' whatever that may mean."[82] *The Times* provided an international dimension when warning of the dangers of censorship; the rising in support of "Ireland's struggle for freedom" was designed to prejudice Americans against Britain and to "make mischief" between the two governments. "Their [the rebels] efforts cannot be regarded with entire indifference, but the remedy lies in the hands of the British cabinet. If they try and hush up any part of the truth, or to confine intelligence reaching America to official communications doled out by themselves, the German agencies in the United States and the Irish 'extremists' will have a field day for their malign activities." *The Daily Mail* attributed self interest to the government's delay in revealing the rising and dismissed Birrell's justification that it was designed to stop the information reaching neutral countries, in particular the United States, where it would be used to create a false impression and exaggerate the importance of the rising. "The answer to this absurd excuse is that they [ministers] ought to have known what was happening in the country and that they did know of several incidents – some of which we have not yet been permitted to publish – that should have set them on the alert. The fact is that they were too busy averting the 'national disaster' of their possible removal from office to be able to attend to anything else."[83] At the weekend, *The Observer* followed these arguments and agreed with Birrell of the need to "confute all

[81] *Observer*, Sunday, 30 April 1916, p8
[82] *The Manchester Guardian*, Wednesday, 26 April 1916, p4
[83] *The Daily Mail*, Tuesday, 25 April 1916, p7

the inevitable exaggerations and falsehood of the German plotters and the Clan na Gael," but deplored the censorship as likely only to make matters worse.[84]

The delay announcing the rising concentrated press coverage over the weekend. Friday's more detailed press statement meant that newspapers devoted multiple pages using material gleaned in the previous few days. *The Daily Mail* provided the most detailed reports including material from correspondents in Ireland. But at this stage it was evident to newspapers that the rising, now contained to Dublin, was all but over and press interest was waning. Some papers dramatised reporting to enliven a flagging story with headlines on unsubstantiated stories like "Movement spreading in the west". That said, this sort of coverage and that of the "wild orgy of drink and loot" was limited to a single day.[85] The popular dailies, now with access to Dublin and to eyewitness accounts, were at their best describing, in the absence of photographs, a graphic picture of the horror of street warfare and destruction of central Dublin.[86] The "tale of Dublin during the past few days reads like a page torn from the history of the French Revolution," said *The Daily Mail*, which, like other papers, presented the story of the rising in the style of war reporting, one already familiar to readers. Its reports included accounts of heroic deeds by British soldiers "bravely and fearlessly" risking their lives to help injured colleagues despite "sniping fire from rooftops and windows".[87] Contemporary papers acknowledged the quality, accuracy and detail of *The Daily Mail*'s reports that were "fuller and better than those in all other papers put together and

[84] *Observer*, Sunday 30 April 1916, p8
[85] *The Daily Mail*, Saturday, 29 April 1916, p3
[86] *The Daily Mirror* published its first photographs showing scenes of devastation in Dublin post the rising in its 2 May 1916 issue and devoted the front page of the 11 May issue to the rebellion but with less dramatic pictures. *The Daily News* ran its first pictures in the 4 May and 5 May issues
[87] *The Daily Mail*, Saturday, 29 April 1916, p9

represented a big feat in newspaper enterprise."[88] Saturday's reporting
corrects some of the errors and misinterpretation in earlier reports with
German involvement now rarely mentioned. *The Manchester Guardian's*
special correspondent noted that the "rebels evidently had a good supply of
ammunition but the great variety of types which have been found rather
goes against the suggestion that it came from Germany... I have seen all
kinds of abandoned weapons, from a fairly modern type of machine rifle to
an air gun, and much of the ammunition appears to have been home-made
in a rather amateurish but very crude form; the shot cartridges have been
charged with heavy slugs, and some of the soft-nosed bullets have been
treated in such a way as to give them the shattering effect of the dum-
dum".[89]

---

[88] *Observer*, Sunday, 30 April 1916, p8
[89] *The Manchester Guardian*, Wednesday, 3 May 1916, p5

5 NEWSPAPER POTRAYALS OF REBELS

THE *OBSERVER*'S report published on the Sunday after the rebellion is a
striking piece of good journalism. The article displays detailed
understanding of Irish politics and places the rebellion within an imperial
context to predict that "good may come out of the Sinn Fein rising not less
than out of the South African revolt".[90] The South African rebellion posed a
serious threat to the fledgling South African government, particularly for its
Afrikaner leaders like Louis Botha and Jan Smuts facing a political challenge
from the Nationalist party led by James Hertzog, a former minister in
Botha's government and, like Botha and Smuts, a former Boer commander.
Likening the two events, *The Observer* said, "The Sinn Feiners are worse
enemies by far to their own country than to the British Empire, and Mr

---

[90] *Observer,* Sunday, 30 April 1916, p8. The rebellion in October 1914 in the Union of South
Africa, then four years old, bore remarkable similarities to the Easter Rising. It started in the
former Afrikaner Republics, led by former Boer commanders, and involved eleven thousand
farmers and bywoners (share-croppers). The trigger was the decision by the South African
government, following a request from London, to invade German South West Africa that
antagonised Afrikaner nationalists sympathetic to Germany for its support of the Afrikaner
republics during the South African War. For a detailed account see T R H Davenport, 'The
South African Rebellion, 1914' *The English Historical Review,* Vol 78, No 306 (Jan 1963) pp
73-94

Redmond is no more responsible for Casement and the Sinn Feiners than General Botha for De Wet and Hertzog. That he will fight as directly and unflinchingly against them we trust and pray."[91] South African references appear frequently in newspaper discussion about the rising with reports of Botha's telegram to Redmond, sent on 29 April, offering his sympathy and regret that "a small section in Ireland had imperilled the great cause".[92] Comparison is also made between the South African government's treatment of its rebels with a single execution and the multiple executions carried out in Ireland.

Lloyds Weekly News, one of a few papers to name the rebel leaders and include their photographs, avoids demonising the rebels, as did the *Observer*[93] or criminalising them, as did *The Manchester Guardian*.[94] A front page of *Lloyds Weekly News* featured, as part of its first coverage of the rising, a large photograph showing Countess Markiewicz preparing food in a soup kitchen to feed striking workers in Dublin during the 1913 unrest.[95] She is described as "Sinn Feiners' titled women leader" and, in an unintentional pun, as a "striking personality" but no mention is made of her wearing military uniform or her active role in the fighting. *Lloyds Weekly News* provided the most positive presentation of the rebel position but the overall tone adopted by all the newspapers in this representative sample, even avowedly Unionist papers, was less hostile than might be expected when compared to newspaper coverage of Afrikaners and their republics

---

[91] *Observer*, Sunday 30 April 1916, p8

[92] *The Daily News and Leader*, Wednesday, 3 May 1916, p5

[93] "They [the rebels] rejoiced in their demented separatism as lunatics might exult in running about amongst the flames of a house they had set on fire." *Observer*, Sunday, 30 April 1916, p8

[94] "Little is known of the crimes committed by the Sinn Feiners in the remote districts, but intelligence has reached Belfast of the murder - for no other term can be used - of a number of members of the Royal Irish Constabulary, including a district inspector." *The Manchester Guardian*, Wednesday, 3 May 1916, p5

[95] *Lloyds Weekly News*, Sunday, 30 April 1916. See appendix 5, page 51 for facsimile

Lloyds Weekly News, Sunday, 30 April 1916
Lloyds Weekly News provided the most positive presentation of the rebel position. It is one of a few papers to name the rebel leaders and include their photographs including this front-page sympathetically showing Countess Markiewicz preparing food in a soup kitchen to feed striking workers in Dublin during the 1913 unrest

during the South African War or that of Germans during the current war. There is none of the lynch-mob mentality that surrounded Casement's arrest with reports of calls in Parliament for his immediate execution. Casement was deemed to be English, despite his Irish birth, so had no excuse for his unpatriotic behaviour unlike the rebels whose Irishness was an explanation. The parliamentary report in *Lloyds Weekly News* that announced the execution of the first of the rebel leaders, Patrick Pearse, Tom Clarke, and Thomas MacDonagh, highlighted questions to the prime minister, not about the rebels, but when Casement would stand trial. [96] Unlike Casement, who was universally condemned as a traitor, liberal newspapers portrayed rebel leaders like Pearce much more sympathetically as having misplaced loyalty.[97]

The Nottingham Journal and Express made unexpectedly moderate comment in a leader about the local regiment, the Sherwood Foresters. It had suffered the "death and wounding of many officers and men" during the fighting in Dublin. Nevertheless, the paper admitted that the whole episode had "demonstrated beyond the possibility of cavil the loyalty and enthusiasm for the common cause of Britain and her allies of the Irish nation in the mass".[98] *The Observer*, echoing the thoughts of many British army officers, believed the fault lay not with the young Irishmen who rebelled but with the lack of firm management of Ireland and insufficient recruitment into the army – failures attributed to the government that displayed "neither candour, courage, nor imagination in the treatment of Irish affairs." Ireland's exemption from conscription frequently appears in coverage of the rising and, in an echo of Redmond's complaint, the

---

[96] *Lloyds Weekly News*, Thursday, 2 May 1916, front page
[97] Pearce is described as "truly an Irishman of Irishmen", *Lloyds Weekly News*, Sunday, 11 June 1916, p5
[98] David G Boyce, 'British Opinion, Ireland, and the War, 1916-1918' *The Historical Journal*, Vol 17 No 3 (Sept 1974) p576

Observer castigates the authorities for failing to make the "deeds of Irish regiments in Flanders and Gallipoli sufficiently known". It also stressed the distinction between Irish rebels and those serving in the army saying, "Not a word must be said to make harder the position of Irish troops whose hearts are torn with wrath and grief. That they have shown valour and fidelity second to none in the Army we need not recall". [99] The effect of the rising on Irish troops was of great concern to the government although this was not mentioned in Birrell's explanation for the delay revealing the news. The *Observer* noted, with its irony presumably not lost on readers, that by "happy coincidence" alongside coverage of the rising was also extensive coverage in all newspapers of the German assault at Loos on the Western Front. [100] Here, at Hulluch, the 16th Irish Division, which included mostly former members of the Irish Volunteers with strong political loyalty to the Irish Parliamentary Party, repelled a German attack that included gas and artillery barrages. [101]

The *Manchester Guardian*'s early hope that "the outbreak will be speedily suppressed and the unhappy men who instigated and took part in it seized and punished" was fulfilled. [102] Even before Major General Sir John Maxwell arrived in Ireland in the early hours of Friday the rising was contained to a limited number of rebel-held buildings. On Tuesday, the army cordoned central Dublin and when reinforcements arrived, began a systematic attack on the various rebel strongholds. On Friday, the GOP and other buildings were demolished with artillery fire and by early afternoon on Saturday the crisis was over when the main contingent of rebels holed up in the remains of the GPO surrendered. The use of artillery

---

[99] *Observer*, Sunday 30 April 1916, p8
[100] 'Huns driven out by Irish' second news lead, *The Daily Mail*, Friday, 28 April 1916, p3
[101] Timothy Bowman, *Irish Regiments in the Great War – Discipline and Morale*, Manchester University Press (Manchester 2003) p124
[102] *The Manchester Guardian*, Wednesday, 26 April 1916, p4

to demolish the buildings held by rebels may have been costly in terms of property – £1million worth of damage and 179 buildings fired[103] – but by avoiding frontal assaults by troops probably kept military deaths to the minimum; 64 rebels and 132 troops and police died during the rebellion.[104] The skill demonstrated by the army is impressive given the relatively untrained British soldiers employed, many hastily called up from the mainland, and the lack of experience by the British army, indeed any army, of urban warfare. A Press Bureau statement issued on Monday, 1 May confirmed what most papers had been saying the previous day and Tuesday's edition of *The Daily News* ran a banner headline, "Unconditional surrender of the Irish rebels". It was the "last of the Irish Republic" and with it went the interest of the great mass of the English public, as interpreted by newspapers, in Irish news. Of more personal interest to most in England was impending conscription for all men between eighteen years and forty one years of age, including married men previously excluded, which lead the news coverage on most of Thursday's editions. The speed with which the rebellion was suppressed along with the government's delay in releasing press statements concentrated press coverage into a five-day window, from Wednesday 26 April to Sunday 30 April. Events "marched fast under a rapid chase of light and darkness"[105] and daily paper coverage had to catch up to keep some sense of continuity and interest to the story they were telling. There was no press comment on the immediate actions to suppress the rising, partly because censorship meant it was over before newspapers could report the event in any detail, and partly because the result had justified the means. Suppression was a military matter and wartime reporting convention and censorship precluded any criticism, at

---

[103] Estimated by Captain Purcell, chief fire officer, Dublin Fire Brigade quoted in Michael Foy and Brian Barton, *The Easter Rising*, Sutton Publishing (Stroud 1999) p324
[104] Michael Foy and Brian Barton, *The Easter Rising*, Sutton Publishing (Stroud 1999) p325
[105] *Observer*, Sunday, 14 May 1916, p8

least initially. Maxwell was in regular contact with the cabinet but with the Irish administration virtually inert – Birrell resigned on 1 May and Nathan on 3 May – he had de facto control of Ireland and exercised his powers swiftly. Following the rising 3,509 men and women were arrested of which 187 were selected for court martial; Countess Markievicz was the only woman to face a court martial.[106] The number arrested, which would have suggested a far larger rising than that which took place, was not reported until much later. Nor were the court martial proceedings, a parody of a legal process, that were held in camera and lasted a matter of a few hours at most. For those sentenced to death, execution took place the following day and was announced by press statement. The trials began on May 2 when Patrick Pearse, Thomas MacDonagh, Thomas Clarke were sentenced to death and shot at first light the next day in Kilmainham jail.[107] The process continued with announcements each day of the executions: on 4 May of Edward Daly, Willie Pearse, Michael O'Hanrahan, Joseph Plunkett; on 5 May of John MacBride; then on 8 May of Richard Kent, Seán Heuston, Eamon Ceannt, Michael Mallin, and Con Colbert. Following a short interval the court martial process resumed and on 12 May when James Connolly and Seán MacDermott were executed at which point Asquith interceded and instructed Maxwell to refer further death sentences to the cabinet.

All papers reported the steady stream of official press statements from Ireland announcing them in a straightforward manner usually with additional background material on each person. Treatment of the stories

---

[106] Michael Foy and Brian Barton, *The Easter Rising*, Sutton Publishing (Stroud 1999) p247
[107] All the executions bar that of Richard Kent, executed in Cork, were carried out in Kilmainham jail and although in 1916 it was little more than a military detention barracks it had huge significance for Irish nationalists because of its close links to defeated Irish rebels: previous prisoners included leaders of the 1798 Rebellion, Robert Emmet in 1803, and it was the place of executions for the five Invincibles in 1882 who killed the Chief Secretary for Ireland. Michael Foy and Brian Barton, *The Easter Rising*, Sutton Publishing (Stroud 1999) p359

was initially low key: *The Daily News* banner headline emphasises Birrell's resignation ahead of the rebels' execution.[108] The news story, running as second lead on the page, reports the execution of three rebel leaders, unnamed, in the first paragraph but with the remainder of the lengthy and detailed story reporting Birrell's speech of the previous evening that followed his resignation and which included his admission that he had seriously underestimated Sinn Féin's strength, membership, and the danger it posed to British rule. Given the sympathetic coverage that *The Daily News* provided of the rebels it is a remarkably muted report of the executions of Patrick Pearse, Tom Clarke, and Thomas MacDonagh following their trial by court martial and suggests only limited public interest in the executions. By contrast, a month later, *Lloyds Weekly News* published a sympathetic story of Pearse, prominently placed and headlined "Condemned rebel chief's farewell to his mother" with a sub-head "How Patrick Pearse met the soldier's death of his desire". Pearse, identified as the most prominent figure in the "pathetic Irish rebellion", is "truly an Irishman of Irishmen". The paper also printed in full his letter written to his mother immediately before his execution and used as evidence against him at his trial by court martial on 2 May.[109] Coverage of Joseph Plunkett's execution is extensive and concentrates on his marriage hours before his execution when "out of the unhappy tragedy of the Sinn Fein rebellion comes a pathetic romance."[110] Likewise, MacBride is given a similarly generous portrait, his military rank is used, and the report includes without any overt criticism details of his service in the Irish brigade fighting for the "Boers" in the South African War. Set against the headlines demeaning Casement as traitor, coverage of rebel leaders is surprisingly positive and

---

[108] *The Daily News and Leader*, Thursday, 4 May 1916, front page
[109] *Lloyds Weekly News*, Sunday, 4 June 1916, p5
[110] *Lloyds Weekly News*, *Sunday*, 7 May 1916, p2

generous. *The Daily News* front page announcement of Countess Markievicz's death sentence and that it was commuted for life provides graphic descriptions of her role at St Stephen's Green, "the last considerable body to surrender" and describes how before handing over her revolver "she kissed it dramatically". *The Daily News* correspondent reported the impact the executions were having in Ireland saying, "up to the present day eight of the rebels have been executed and 63 sent to penal servitude... The news of the executions makes gloomy reading in the [Irish] papers, all of which are now appearing once more. The rebels who are shot are blindfolded when called upon to face the firing party, but one or two have demanded the privilege of going to their death with open eyes and I understand that the request has been granted."[111]

---

[111] *The Daily News*, Monday, 8 May 1916, front page in a report from Dublin by Hugh Martin, the *Daily Mirror's* special correspondent. Martin would become better known to English readers for his reporting of the Irish War on Independence immediately after the war

6 NEWSPAPER LANGUAGE

THE LANGUAGE used in many of the these press reports about the executions emphasises the military nature of the proceedings talking of court martial, execution by firing squad, privileges for the condemned, and use of military rank as in the case of Major MacBride. It evokes the heroisms of defeated soldiers, and not, as some would have preferred, the image of criminal rebels responsible for murder. That these men are military leaders whose valour, even if in the wrong cause, must be recognised is implicit in these newspaper reports. "There was misguided chivalry in the Sinn Fein rising – courage and height of soul are the common property of Europe and beyond in these times – but there was enough ugliness as well as folly to spoil Mr Dillon's false romance."[112] Dillon's speech to the Commons on 11 May denouncing the executions, witheringly dismissed by the *Observer* as an exultation of the courage and skill of the Sinn Féin insurgents, received widespread coverage although little was made by newspapers of the heckling by English members of parliament that seems out of keeping with the tone adopted by most

---

[112] *The Observer*, Sunday, 14 May 1916, p9

newspapers towards the executions. Asquith's surprise announcement of his planned visit to Ireland did much to deflect criticism of his handling of the crisis and took precedence in newspaper coverage. "What promised to be a fierce debate on the military executions in Ireland flickered out this evening on the announcement by the Prime Minister of his imminent departure for Dublin."[113] Newspaper coverage of Ireland had, by this stage returned to its pre-war pattern determined more by parliamentary debate than events in Ireland. But not entirely, as newspapers were now also reporting the case of Francis Sheehy-Skeffington, shot while under arrest by a junior army officer on Tuesday 25 April. His widow, unsatisfied with the perfunctory enquiry that vindicated the officer, had campaigned with support from the *Freeman's Journal* for a public inquiry into the circumstances of the death of Sheehy-Skeffington and the two other men executed with him.[114] A court martial was agreed which Asquith insisted should be in public. *The Daily Mirror* used Asquith's comment, that the "Skeffington case seems to be an inexcusable act"[115] as the banner headline for its story that included a report on Dillon's speech. News of the Sheehy-Skeffington execution and court martial, coming on top of the executions taking place that week, raised the prospect that if relatively junior offices were empowered under martial law to conduct executions, as the Sheehy-Skeffington execution suggested, there were likely to be many more as yet undisclosed. Asquith's inability or unwillingness to emphatically state that there had been no other similar executions only fuelled concern. *The Daily Mirror*'s story linked the court martial executions with that of Sheehy-Skeffington and included details of a letter in *The Manchester Guardian* saying that he was arrested while posting placards calling upon the people

---

[113] *The Daily Mail*, Friday, 12 May 1916, p5
[114] *The Daily Mirror*, Thursday, 11 May 1916, p2
[115] *The Daily Mirror*, Friday, 12 May 1916, p2

to desist from looting. Mrs Skeffington is quoted as saying that her husband was "unarmed and a non-combatant".[116] However, the author Arnold Bennett, in his regular column in *The Daily News* probably caught the public mood regarding Sheehy-Skeffington's execution when he said, "I greatly regret the manner of his death, but a pacifist he was not".[117] The Sheehy-Skeffington case undoubtedly had more impact in Dublin where he was well known, than in England's national press more concerned with the court martial executions. In contrast to its often-strident tone of commentary, *The Daily Mail* provided only muted support of the executions believing "it inevitable that the leaders of such a movement should be dealt with promptly and severely". It distinguished between the court martial executions and that of Sheehy-Skeffington, on which it reserved judgement pending the outcome of the promised inquiry. *The Daily Mail* editorial lacks the paper's usual outspoken confidence and, unusual for the paper, it publishes alongside a leader supporting executions an eight hundred-word letter – twice the length of the editorial – from George Bernard Shaw. He contradicts *The Daily Mail*'s assertion made on 9 May that "so far as the leaders are concerned no voice has been raised in this country against the infliction of the punishment which has so speedily overtaken them".[118] Papers like *The Times* and *Observer* always qualified their support for the court martial process and executions. Both papers endorsed the home secretary, Herbert Samuel's statement that the "revolt was marked by several cold blooded, deliberate murders of policemen and of civilians, and the Government would have been guilty of unpardonable weakness if they had not meted out stern penalties".[119] Indeed most newspapers express this argument in one form or another; however, *The Times* believed that

---

[116] *The Daily Mirror*, Thursday 11 May 1916, p2
[117] *The Daily News and Leader,* Monday, 29 May 1916, p4
[118] *The Daily Mail*, Wednesday, 10 May 1916, p4
[119] *The Daily Mirror*, Thursday, 11 May, p2

"government has been foolish in not stating plainly the reason why these men were shot".[120] For the *Observer*, "Not for a moment can it be considered that the punishment of the fourteen [sic] leaders who were shot was excessive," the fault lay in the process, "execution by driblets" that "day by day spreads out until the effect on Irish feeling became harrowing, exasperating, unendurable as though hundreds were being doomed by pitilessness of cold power".[121]

The *Manchester Guardian* was far more critical in a series of ever more strident and passionate leaders from 6 May. The first executions were condemned: "Enough – more than enough – has been done for example and warning.... No doubt these men have rendered themselves liable to the death penalty, but then so have many hundreds, even thousands of other men. Dublin is full of them."[122] This latter claim sits uncomfortably with the *Manchester Guardian's* endorsement the previous week that the rising had the support of only a handful of extremists. However, *The Manchester Guardian's* most powerful criticism, as far as the government was concerned, was is accusation that government had allowed the military to take control. "They have done their work courageously and well. But the question of retribution is one involving considerations of policy which it is for statesmen to determine." *The Manchester Guardian* cites Carson's call for "coolness and deliberation" to support its argument warning that "if from weakness or carelessness the cabinet seeks to shuffle off its responsibility on to the shoulders of the soldiers, it may be laying up for the future in the hearts of Irishmen the seeds of misfortune as great as those which are now our sorrow and shame".[123] By May 9 after the execution of Kent, Heuston, Ceannt, Mallin, and Colbert, *The Manchester Guardian* called the

[120] *The Times*, Friday, 12 May 12 1916, p 9
[121] *Observer*, Sunday 14 May 1916, p8
[122] *The Manchester Guardian*, Saturday 6 May 1916, p6
[123] *The Manchester Guardian*, Saturday 6 May 1916 p6

executions "an atrocity" and deplored Asquith's failure to pledge an end to these, especially in light of Redmond's plea in Parliament for clemency.

The Manchester Guardian campaign against executions also highlighted the anomaly of Casement, in prison in England awaiting a civil trial. *The Manchester Guardian* contrasted the impending trial of Casement, as much a ringleader as the others, in a civil court in England with those who had faced "military tribunals sitting in private without any of the ordinary safeguards of justice".[124] The cabinet had decided as early as 27 April that he would face trial in open civil court rather than a court martial. Press coverage of his trial all but overshadowed that of the Royal Commission chaired by Lord Hardinge into the rising. The hearings started on 18 May 1916 but produced no headline-making revelations although newspapers ran a steady stream of down page stories, notably on American sources of funding for Sinn Féin [125] and active support of "young Irish catholic priests" for the rebellion.[126] It was Casement's trial, not the hearings that became the focus for English papers the moment he appeared at Bow Street Magistrates Court on 15 May for committal proceedings. The case was rarely off news pages: detailed reports described Casement's landing, along with two former British soldiers, from a submarine on the coast of County Kerry; the attempted landing of guns by the German auxiliary; and testimony from a diver who had inspected the wreck scuttled by its German crew near Cork harbour. In an earlier report the *Observer* contrasted the "bravery and vigour of the determined act by the German crew of the gun running vessel" with the "singularly artless botch of his [Casement] share of the business".[127] The trial would confirm this assessment of Casement. Although the first newspaper reports of his arrest

---

[124] *The Manchester Guardian*, Tuesday, 9 May1916, p4
[125] *The Daily Mirror*, Friday, 19 May 1916, p2
[126] *Lloyds Weekly News*, Sunday, 21 May 1916, p7
[127] *Observer*, Sunday, 30 April, 1916, p8

typically included strong adjectives like "traitor " or "renegade" these disappear in later reports when he is depicted less as villain more that of a misguided fool. Newspapers highlight his compassion talking of how Casement "sobbed on hearing the news of the drowning at Killorglin of two men" when under arrest and being escorted to Dublin. *The Daily Mirror* described him on the second day in court as "in more serious mood than the previous day" and how he "pressed his solicitor's hand in his own as if to emphasise some point he had made". Also appearing in the case and standing in the dock alongside Casement was Daniel Bailey, one of the two former soldiers who travelled with Casement from Germany by submarine.[128] In some press reports, Bailey is frequently contrasted unfavourably with Casement with reference to Casement's "neat attire" and Bailey's "unshaven appearance".[129]

Newspaper interest in the case flagged once the initial revelations were published, a reflection of the general consensus among most newspaper readers that a guilty verdict was a certainty, and war reporting returned to lead news pages. On May 16 *The Daily Mirror* lead its news with "French drive foe from 220 yards of trenches on Meuse heights" with Casement taking second lead the following day. *The Daily News* pushed the Casement trial to second lead in favour of "Irish regiment avenges German taunts on Ireland" reporting how the 8th Royal Munster Fusiliers captured a poster raised by the Germans taunting the Irish about English troops firing on Irish women while suppressing the rising.[130] But declining public interest was not reflected in cabinet where the death sentence was

---

[128] Robert Monteith and Daniel Bailey, former British soldiers captured during fighting on the Western front by the German army were released to join Casement's Irish Brigade, and travelled with Casement to Ireland. Monteith evaded capture and fled to the US

[129] *The Daily Mirror*, Wednesday, 17 May 1916, p3

[130] *The Daily News*, Wednesday May 17, front page. Some battalions made a point of demonstrating their opposition to the rising. The 9th Royal Munster Fusiliers hung an effigy of Casement in no man's land. Timothy Bowman, *Irish Regiments in the Great War – Discipline and Morale*, Manchester University Press (Manchester 2003) p129

the subject of debate on several occasions. The home secretary, Herbert Samuel, required that the full cabinet determine whether the prerogative of mercy should be exercised. Some members including Asquith believed that he should be kept in confinement as a criminal lunatic, however expert opinion declared him "abnormal but not certifiably insane" and the cabinet decided he should be hanged.[131]

---

[131] Michael Foy and Brian Barton, *The Easter Rising*, Sutton Publishing (Stroud 1999) p376

7 CHANGING PUBLIC OPINION

AS WITH the execution of the Irish rebel leaders, Irish public opinion was
not an issue although on this the cabinet may well have been justified as
there is little evidence to suggest Casement's enjoyed much public support
in Ireland. In England Casement's execution met with little public
opposition. *The Daily Mirror,* commenting on the sentence said "the point
is that at a time when France and we fight for freedom and *against* [sic]
oppression, this man stood up for tyranny, and helped the oppressor – then
with a ghastly hypocrisy, poised as a 'liberator' to the lambs he led towards
the slaughter. That is what it is impossible to forgive".[132] A campaign
developed, supported by *The Manchester Guardian,* to argue the case for
clemency but *The Manchester Guardian's* leader columns lacked the
passion that featured so strongly in its efforts to stop the court martial
executions in Ireland. It argued that Casement's writing demonstrated his

---

[132] *The Daily Mirror,* 30 June 1916, p5

distinction between fighting for Ireland and fighting on the side of Germany. "That a man of keen intelligence, with passionate love of freedom and impulsive generosity of temperament, in the middle of a war like this, should hold to Germany to be a friend and England the enemy of freedom that he loved, must seem indeed a strange thing, and would be unintelligible apart from the memory of ancient wrongs over which his spirit brooded. Sentence of death has been passed upon this strange and perverse spirit. The death penalty will do nothing to kill such dreams; rather it will give them life. For the sake of the new Ireland which we hope to see, it is a moment for clemency."[133]

The Manchester Guardian distinguished between the cases of the leaders of the rebellion shot immediately after the suppression arguing that for those who think their execution a blunder does not justify, on the basis of equal treatment, that Casement too should be executed. "The rebellion is now well over and we are dealing w
ith a question of punishment...In the present case what is at stake is the relation between Great Britain and Ireland, upon which the relations of the British Empire and the United States in large measure depend...the reverse of all these things is the effect reasonably to be expected from his execution." The newspaper argued that it was "the difference between an act done in the haste and heat of self defence and an act done with full deliberation in time of safety".[134]

The campaign against Casement's execution had little support among national newspapers but equally there was no strong counter case argued in the press, which is probably a reasonable reflection of English public opinion not overly concerned about a decision that was the product of a fair trial. The day following the passing of the death sentence on Casement,

---

[133] *The Manchester Guardian*, Friday, 30 June 1916, p6
[134] *The Manchester Guardian*, Wednesday, 19 July 1916, p4

the *Liverpool Echo*, which covered the case in great detail, reported how Casement's "long and irrelevant speech was borne by the judges with admirable patience.... utterly illogical and nothing to do with the case, full latitude was given to the pathetic figure in the dock to express himself to address the outside world for the last time."[135]

The Manchester Guardian's final appeal was directly to the cabinet, but most likely specifically to Asquith: "the government have decided that Roger Casement shall be executed today. By doing so they will have missed a rare opportunity of showing that wisdom of magnanimity which distinguishes the statesman from the politician... Of a man discredited otherwise before the world they will have made a martyr to live in the long traditions of Irishmen at home and abroad. They will have set at nought the very unusual requests of the senate of the United States, disregarding utterly sentiments of a nation on whose goodwill much depends. They had eyes and ears for nothing but the hot resentment of the present, that clamour for blood which rises so vehemently in times of excitement from normally placable and kindly men. It is strange that everyone can appreciate the blended wisdom and nobility of general Botha's treatment of De Wet, everyone can understand the stupidity of the execution of Italy's rebels by Austria, everyone is proud of acts of clemency in our past history, and feels the awkwardness of apologizing for severity and ruthlessness, yet so few can apply the lesson here and now."[136]

It was not Casement who would become the martyr for Irish nationalism, the government smear campaign using his diaries probably did most to destroy that, but this leader in *The Manchester Guardian* accurately portrayed the result that the executions of Irish rebel leaders would have in Ireland. Casement was executed on 3 August, the second anniversary of

---

[135] *Liverpool Echo*, Tuesday, 30 June 1916
[136] *The Manchester Guardian*, Thursday, 3 August 1916, p4

the war, at Pentonville prison.[137] For English newspapers the "execution of Roger Casement, ex Knight and British consular official, as a traitor to his country at a time of her greatest trial, brings to a close one of the most remarkable episodes of the war." [138]

---

[137] *The Daily Mirror,* Friday, 28 July 1916, p2 reported, with a hint of regret, that there was no truth in suggestions that the 1866 statute abolishing public executions excluded high treason and that Casement would be hanged in public
[138] *Liverpool Echo,* Thursday, 3 August 1916

8 INTERNATIONAL DIMENSIONS

THE EASTER RISING was more than just a purely Irish event; the implications for Home Rule meant government responded more to British, and even American public opinion, than to Irish. Its failure to adequately manage media coverage for these audiences, which stemmed from the ineptness of the Irish Administration, would also have lasting consequences for Ireland. The rebels had chosen to declare a republic and had formed "the armed propaganda of a self elected vanguard which claimed the power to interpret the general will."[139] The government met the challenge in Ireland with physical force of the military and, equally as crude, its powers under the Defence of the Realm Act, to suppress newspapers in Ireland.[140]

---

[139] Charles Townshend, *Easter 1916 – The Irish Rebellion,* Penguin Books (London 2006) p312
[140] Statutory censorship power was available in the form of the Defence of the Realm Act with Regulations 18, 27, and 51 applying to the press. Regulation 51 referred to the need to "prevent the spread of false reports or reports likely to cause disaffection to His Majesty or to interfere with the success of His Majesty's forces by land or sea or to prejudice His Majesty's relations with foreign powers". Regulation 18 prohibited obtaining and communicating naval and military information. This covered most aspects of the work done by the official Press Bureau and gave the 'voluntary' censorship the support of statutory compulsion. Unfavourable newspaper opinion was dealt with by regulation 27, which reiterated the intention to prevent the spread of 'false reports' likely to cause 'disaffection' and was the most frequently used when prosecuting dissidents

But England's influential national newspapers required a more subtle approach that government never managed to achieve. Media management depends on having enough information that when skilfully released sets the tone of media reports and sustains the desired direction of newspaper coverage. Although the British government regained the initiative taken by the rebels when they occupied key buildings in Dublin and declared a republic, in media terms it was never able to fully take advantage. Instead, government, in much the same way as it abdicated its power and responsibility to the army in Ireland, allowed newspapers to dictate coverage of the rising.

The cabinet had thirty-two hours between notification of the first shots fired in the rising and its public announcement in Parliament. That should have been ample time to establish the scale and extent of the rising, formulate a response, prepare a detailed press statement, and privately brief newspaper editors. However, there was a critical lack of information from the Irish administration. In that thirty-two hour period, General W H M Lowe took command of military forces in Ireland and set in motion orders for troop movements and reinforcements. It appears that Lowe had no predetermined plan to follow and improvised, effectively as it transpired, but presumably based on intelligence about rebel positions. General Friend, on leave in England when the rising started, but who took command when he arrived in Kingstown (Dún Laoghaire) at nine on the Tuesday morning, followed Lowe's tactics.[141] By contrast, the civil authorities, on which the government relied, were in almost complete disarray. Nathan was isolated in Dublin Castle, Birrell was in London, and Lord Wimborne, the Lord Lieutenant and principally a figurehead for the administration, based himself in the Viceregal Lodge, his official residence in Phoenix Park, some three miles from Dublin Castle. Despite the proximity, Wimborne had poor communication with the Castle and declared martial law in Dublin without consulting the Attorney General or other legal officers.[142] His decision was unnecessary in that the military had not felt constrained taking control of the situation without such power, but would have far reaching consequences as it effectively handed the Irish administration to the military; the last time that had happened in Ireland was during the 1798 rebellion. For some weeks before the rising Wimborne had issued all manner of warnings about impending trouble but at the critical moment was unable to provide any useful function within the civil administration. Crucially there appears to have been no co-ordinated effort by the civil authorities to gather information; a priority in this situation, certainly for London. A message from the military reporting the situation in Dublin was sent at 1.10 pm on Monday to the Naval Centre at Kingstown and transmitted to London by wireless. And by noon on Tuesday the military had control of the Castle so Nathan was in a position to communicate with London using despatch riders and wireless. Despite the weakness of British intelligence in Ireland with un-coordinated multiple intelligence gathering organisations identified by The Royal Commission[143] intelligence, in Dublin at least, appears to have been good. On the Monday, after three unarmed Dublin Metropolitan Police officers were killed the entire force was taken off the streets. The Commissioner then put them in plain clothes and sent them out scouting when they provided a stream of information about rebel movements. By Monday night, the military was well appraised of the situation but not Birrell in London. On Tuesday evening the government issued its short and inconsistent Press Bureau statement. At this point, it lost the advantage in terms of media control. Birrell's statement was carefully

---

[142] Charles Townshend, *Easter 1916 – The Irish Rebellion,* Penguin Books (London 2006) p187
[143] Charles Townshend, *Easter 1916 – The Irish Rebellion,* Penguin Books (London 2006) p25

worded and the government would have known how it would be used by the press, particularly the Sinn Féin reference. The similarity of much of the initial speculation in the press points to private briefings of editors. In the fevered atmosphere prevailing in 1916, with German invasion threats a real possibility, and not just in the public mind as testimony by military personnel at the Royal Commission[144] showed, it is easy to see how readers, as well as well-briefed leader writers and editors, would connect German military activity with the rising. Press themes, portraying the rising as part of a concerted German plot against Britain with Casement playing a key role as rebel leader, dominated the first reports of the rising: suppressing the rising was a military campaign to thwart German plans rather than suppressing Irish nationalism and this was the line most papers adopted, even Unionist papers that offered Redmond's constitutional nationalists considerable support. Information was in circulation that some sort of display would be made over the weekend especially in light of planned parades by Volunteers. In that sense, the rising was not unexpected. Government chose to delay for as long as possible any announcement of the rising on the basis that it would turn out to be a minor affair; and despite the damage to central Dublin it could well have been portrayed as such to English audiences. Birrell's justification for the delay, that government wished to ensure that no news reach neutral countries, especially the United States, that would exaggerate the significance of the rising, makes sense in this respect. Nevertheless, English newspapers were suspicious, especially Unionist papers, that this was a government attempt to conceal the true extent of the rising and earlier attempts to limit press reporting of parliamentary and cabinet debate fuelled this.

The government failed to take advantage of the speed of the

---

[144] Charles Townshend, *Easter 1916 – The Irish Rebellion,* Penguin Books (London 2006) p183

suppression, made shorter for the English public by the delay in reporting its outbreak. Military success in crushing the rising was a stroke of good fortune for the government but squandered. English newspapers, in the appropriate wartime spirit that they were well used to, provided generous coverage of the successful military performance, and of how proficient British soldiers, many of them Irish, had fought bravely to suppress the rising. It was at this stage that the Irish administration should have taken control. But the implosion of the Irish Civil Administration, and Wimborne's decision to impose martial law, meant Maxwell filled the power vacuum, and encouraged by Field Marshal Kitchener, Secretary of State for War, embarked on his court martial process with its steady, day by day, tally of executions.[145] Instead of press statements detailing the return to normality, newspapers were fed a succession of executions, all duly reported with growing unease and not solely from liberal sections of the media. The government lost the opportunity to close newspaper coverage of the rising; instead reporting was maintained providing greater coverage of the rebels and their nationalist ideals. Much as *The Manchester Guardian* warned, executions created martyrs and provided nationalism with the "oxygen of publicity" as a later British premier would complain in not dissimilar circumstances.[146] Up until the weekend it was still possible to dismiss the rising as a large-scale street riot but once the execution process got underway on 2 May that opportunity was lost. The apparently unlimited number of executions that was likely to take place meant the rebellion was now perceived as major political event. Clearly the government failed to consider the consequences of the process and allowing the court martial to take place is at odds with the decision made

---

[145] Michael Foy and Brian Barton, *The Easter Rising*, Sutton Publishing (Stroud 1999) p369
[146] "We must try to find ways to starve the terrorist and the hijacker of the oxygen of publicity on which they depend." Margaret Thatcher in a speech to the American Bar Association in London, 15 July 1985

on 26 April that Casement would be tried in a civil court. Casement's high profile required cabinet attention, unlike the rebels leaders whom it felt could be left to the military machine now in control of much of Ireland, and a reflection of how little attention was placed on Irish public opinion that would have been better served if all rebels leaders had faced a civil trial, even held in England, instead of Maxwell's semi arbitrary court martial process.

Government responded to public opinion as interpreted by newspapers as well as that interpreted by members of parliament: it also had to consider the effect of the rising on serving soldiers, especially Irish soldiers. The heckling John Dillon's speech received from English MPs would certainly have coloured Asquith's judgement regarding executions skewing his assessment towards that of the Commons rather than of newspapers, possibly more attuned to public opinion in this case. There was no war-lust attitude in newspaper reporting of the rising and its aftermath, a measure of general war weariness that prevailed at the time. The campaign to stop the executions led by *The Manchester Guardian* is an expression of this and although Unionist newspapers did not support the campaign, equally, they did not castigate it, and their support for the executions was always qualified. Asquith's decision to announce an end to the executions came too late, appearing reactive rather than decisive. His surprise announcement to visit Ireland to consult "first hand with the civil and military authorities" defused parliamentary criticism but produced little other benefit.[147] Asquith dithered over Casement's execution and government concern over public opinion, especially in the United States, was sufficient to warrant a smear campaign against Casement with unofficial circulation of extracts from his diaries containing evidence of his

---

[147] *The Daily Mirror*, Friday, 12 May 1916, p3

homosexuality. English public opinion appears to have been quite settled on the justification of Casement's execution. His involvement in Germany and attempt to recruit an Irish brigade was a key factor in Casement's trial as portrayed by most newspapers, and with the exception of *The Manchester Guardian*, the justification for his execution. By contrast, English newspapers abandoned the overt German connection, of which they made so much initially, in coverage of the rebel executions. Instead, they were portrayed as defeated military leaders paying the ultimate price for their misguided deeds. In 1914 newspapers had not hesitated to portray Germany and Germans in the worst possible light: looting, murder, rape, and pillage, destruction of cultural and religious buildings were vividly highlighted, true or otherwise but there is no corresponding portrayal, in such negative terms, of Irish rebels, quite the opposite in many cases. Newspapers all carried stories of looting in Dublin but this generally appeared only once. The strongest case against the rebels, made by *The Times* and *The Manchester Guardian,* is limited to early reports when they are described as criminal and occasionally murderers. However, by the end of the week the picture in liberal papers especially, is more of a group of poorly armed, misguided Irish patriots, displaying valour and honour trying to achieve the impossible for their country. For English readers, newspapers suggest Ireland was a country in need of better management and firm discipline, not ruthless suppression.

The attention span of English readers for matters Irish was short. While the rising catapulted Irish affairs on to English newspapers, the successful suppression meant the topic was dropped in favour of war reporting of the summer offensives. For English audiences Casement's execution brought closure while Lloyd George repeated Asquith's 1914 success and put Ireland on the long finger for the duration of the war once more. Unlike

Asquith, English newspapers, including Unionist supporting papers, showed a far greater understanding of Irish public opinion, recognising the damage that Maxwell's military regime was doing in Ireland. The Unionist journalist, Warre B Wells complained that government "made no attempt to explain the real gravity of the Rebellion, but inspired the English press to treat it merely as a sort of street riot on an extensive scale".[148] Had Asquith's government sustained this line, which required returning Ireland to civil control quickly, Irish public opinion may well have mirrored that of the English.

---

[148] Charles Townshend, *Easter 1916 – The Irish Rebellion,* Penguin Books (London 2006) p307

9 ABOUT THE NEWSPAPERS

THIS BOOK examines reporting and commentary from a representative sample of English newspapers; The *Daily Mail, The Daily Mirror, The Daily News, Liverpool Echo, Lloyds Weekly News, The Manchester Guardian, Observer,* and *The Times.* A short biography of each newspaper relevant to 1916 is shown below. The newspapers represent a cross section of political opinion from high circulation, mass appeal papers as well as those with smaller circulations, aimed at smaller, better-educated audiences. The labels Liberal, Unionist, and Independent are crude shorthand and do not reflect the nuances in newspapers political opinion: *The Daily Mirror,* ostensibly independent until Rothermere's influence at the end of the war, was socially aware and supported Liberal causes although not necessarily the Liberal party; Similarly with the *Observer,* that was independent but with strong Unionist sympathies. The labels tabloid, quality, and broadsheet, are used to denote physical size and design and are not judgements about editorial quality and accuracy: during this period at least, good journalism and bad journalism were equally at home in the "quality" *Times* or the "popular" *Daily Mirror.*

The Daily Mail

Circulation   1,172,214
Ownership   Associated Newspapers Limited (Lord Northcliffe)
Editor   Thomas Marlowe
Political support   Unionist

Alfred and Harold Harmsworth launched *The Daily Mail in 1896* with a start up cost of £15,000. The first issue sold out its 397,215 print run and heralded the era of mass appeal newspapers in the UK.[149] The Mail is a broadsheet but by comparison with established titles like *The Times* uses bolder headlines, photographs, and short, sharply written stories. Posters advertising the first issue announced, "Four leading articles, a page of Parliament and columns of speeches will NOT [sic] be found in the Daily Mail."[150] Priced at a halfpenny, *The Daily Mail* was an outstanding success in the pre-war years, in terms of growth and profit. The South African War boosted circulation to the half million mark with the paper taking an extremely nationalistic jingoistic stance. In 1905, Associated Newspapers was formed and ownership transferred to the company under Alfred's control, now Lord Northcliffe. The editor, Thomas Marlowe, was for all practical purposes nominal with Northcliffe directing the paper's content closely. It was a strident Unionist supporting paper within the constraints of Northcliffe's very personal unionist and imperialist views. His financial resources gave the *Daily Mail* and *The Times*, which he purchased in 1908, a degree of independence from government and political parties few papers possessed at the time. Northcliffe waged a relentless campaign criticising Asquith's wartime

---

[149] Daily Mail and General Trust: www.dmgt.co.uk/aboutdmgt/dmgthistory
[150] George Boyce, 'The Fourth Estate: the reappraisal of a concept', in G Boyce, J Curran, P Wingate, eds, *Newspaper History - From the 17thC to the Present Day*, Constable and Company (London 1978) pp24

government, so much so his successor, Lloyd George invited
Northcliffe to join the cabinet. He refused, unlike his newly ennobled
brother, Harold, now Lord Rothermere, who later joined the cabinet.

The Daily Mirror

Circulation	1,200,000
Ownership	Pictorial Newspaper Company Ltd
	(Lord Rothermere)
Editor	E D Flynn
Political support	Independent (but with Liberal leanings)

The Daily Mirror was launched in November 1903, priced at a penny,
as the first daily newspaper for "gentlewomen" by Northcliffe with
Britain's first women newspaper editor, Mary Howarth.[151] The launch
cost an unprecedented £100,000 – £8m at today's prices –- and
included a large promotional campaign. Despite this, sales slumped to
25,653[152] within two months and the more experienced Hamilton Fyfe
replaced Howarth, who was always intended to be a temporary editor.
He resurrected the title, helped by a price reduction to half a penny
and sales boomed enabling it to claim in July 1914 to have "the
world's largest circulation"; in UK terms it was certainly one of the
highest circulations rivalled only by The Daily Mail. Fyfe established
the paper's social awareness, campaigning for causes like child poverty
and social deprivation and in 1907 broadly supporting suffragettes. In
January 1914, Northcliffe sold the Mirror to his brother, Lord
Rothermere, and in 1916, now edited by E D Flynn, an American, it

---

[151] It was 1998 before the second women editor was appointed; Rosie Boycott of The
Daily Express
[152] Bill Hagerty, Read all about it! 100 sensational years of the Daily Mirror, First Stone
Publishing, (Lydney, Gloucestershire 2003) p11

was thriving but with a less Liberal tone. *The Daily Mirror* was a tabloid format paper with very modern design by contemporary standards, much more so than the *Mail*, using bold headlines, front-page pictures and focussed news stories. It used photography to great effect, the very early editions were called *The Illustrated Daily Mirror*, with pictures often as full-page covers, especially during the war when it featured dramatic images like those taken on board the sinking French liner, Sontay, when torpedoed in May 1917.

The Daily News

Circulation	550,000
Ownership	Daily News Ltd (Cadbury family)
Editor	Alfred G Gardiner
Political support	Liberal

The Daily News, founded in 1846 with Charles Dickens as its first editor, had well-established radical roots. A syndicate that included Lloyd George but controlled by the Liberal supporting Cadbury family purchased it in 1901 during the South African War. Edited by Alfred Gardiner who recruited talented writers to the staff, sales grew and after amalgamation with the *Morning Leader* in 1912 the circulation passed the half million mark but was never profitable as a business venture. In 1916, the broadsheet design was imaginative with bold headlines and standfirsts as well as extensive use of photographs.

Liverpool Echo

Circulation	50,000 estimate
Ownership	The Liverpool Daily Post and Echo Ltd (Jeanes family)
Political support	Independent
Editor	Proprietor edited

The *Liverpool Echo* has been included in the sample for this dissertation as representative of English regional papers specifically because of the diverse population mix in Liverpool with a large proportion of Irish, as well as Scots and Welsh within the newspaper's catchment area during this period. The Jeanes family owned the paper and, as was typical at the time of many regional newspapers, editorship was by family members directing the efforts of a senior sub-editor. Politically it adopted a neutral tone with coverage of the Easter Rising more balanced by comparison with national papers like the *Mail* and *Mirror* presumably because of wider Irish-origin readership. Physically the largest paper in this sample, it was printed on approximately A1, and had a traditional, text-heavy design with few photographs.

Lloyds Weekly News

Circulation	1,250,000
Ownership	United Newspapers Limited Frank Lloyd
Editor	Robert Donald
Political support	Liberal

In 1916, *Lloyd's Weekly News*, originally *Lloyd's Illustrated London Newspaper* when launched in 1842, was a Liberal supporting Sunday owned by Frank Lloyd's United Newspapers Ltd and edited by Robert Donald, better known as editor of the *Daily Chronicle*. The paper appealed to the taste and interests of the lower and middle classes whose more limited leisure time created a preference for reading Sunday newspapers.[153] By 1914, circulation was in the region of 1,250,000, slightly behind the market leader, the *News of the World*, which placed more emphasis on sex, crime, and scandal stories. *Lloyd's Weekly News* had by contemporary standards a modern design, not dissimilar to *The Daily News,* with bold headlines, standfirsts and extensive photography.

The Manchester Guardian

Circulation	40-50,000 (estimate)
Ownership	Charles P Scott
Editor	Charles P Scott
Political support	Liberal

The Manchester Guardian, a regional newspaper with circulation concentrated in the northwest and funded by large advertising revenue derived from its position as the commercial organ for the cotton trade,

---

[153] John M McEwen, 'The National Press during the First World War: Ownership and Circulation' *Journal of Contemporary History*, 1982, Vol 17, p470

was more than a Liberal match for *The Times* wielding enormous
influence in London. C P Scott, the editor since 1872, and who
remained in the post until 1929 purchased the paper in 1907. Scott
was also Liberal Member of Parliament for Leigh, Lancashire from
1895 until 1906 and well connected with leading Liberal party figures,
particularly Lloyd George and Lord Loreburn. In 1916, *The
Manchester Guardian*, like *The Times* targeted an educated, influential
readership and used a traditional, type-heavy design with minimal
headlining, and almost no photographs. However, the drab
appearance, even for the time, could not conceal the quality of writing
from excellent staff writers who spoke authoritatively on both national
and international issues.

Observer

Circulation	175,000
Ownership	Waldorf Astor
Editor	James L Garvin
Political support	Unionist

The national Sunday press played an important role in British
journalism in the first half of the 20th century, particularly after 1914
when they became very popular, especially with lower income groups
with leisure time on a Sunday, providing the large circulation of papers
like the *Lloyds Weekly News*. The *Observer*, like the *Sunday Times*
appealed to a smaller, usually better educated, and more influential
readership, but also enjoyed rising sales. J L Garvin, the editor of the
Observer in 1916, although he always referred to himself as "editor

and manager,"[154] was regarded by contemporaries as staunchly independent and was helped in this by funding from the *Observer's* wealthy owner, Waldorf Astor. He inherited the paper from his father who had acquired it in 1911 from Lord Northcliffe when it was floundering with circulation at about 2,000. Garvin, appointed in 1908 by Northcliffe, remained on the paper after the sale and transformed it within two years of joining, to create a new pattern of Sunday paper with longer, magazine style articles expressing distinctive opinions, usually but by no means exclusively, of a Unionist flavour. A small staff meant the paper relied on wire services for news along with Garvin's extensive network of friends, predominantly Conservatives but by 1916, also including figures likes Lloyd George, Beaverbrook, and Churchill.[155]

The Times

Circulation	137,000
Ownership	Associated Newspapers Limited (Lord Northcliffe)
Editor	Geoffrey Dawson
Political support	Unionist

The circulation and reputation of *The Times,* which had been declining since 1870, was brought to a new low in March 1887 with its sustained attempt to destroy the career of Charles Parnell, leader of the Irish Parliamentary Party, using Richard Pigott's forged letter implicating Parnell in the Phoenix Park murders. Parnell sued for libel

---

[154] John Stubbs, 'Appearance and reality: a case study of the Observer and J L Garvin 1914-42' in G Boyce, J Curran, P Wingate, eds, *Newspaper History - From the 17thC to the Present Day*, Constable and Company (London 1978) p324

[155] John Stubbs, 'Appearance and reality: a case study of the Observer and J L Garvin 1914-42' in G Boyce, J Curran, P Wingate, eds, *Newspaper History - From the 17thC to the Present Day*, Constable and Company (London 1978) p329

and *The Times* settled out of court. By the turn of the century, its editorials and reporting mirrored its dull, leaden, and dated design all of which changed following Northcliffe's acquisition in 1908. He instigated an almost complete change of staff under a new editor, Geoffrey Robinson, to rejuvenate the content and, with two price reductions taking it down a penny in 1914, circulation recovered to 183,000 that year.

English newspapers - Ownership and political allegiances

IN 1916, Britain's national newspaper network, comprising more than thirty newspapers and journals, was unequalled in the world for its market penetration and proportionate size of reading audience. But newspapers were not independent and every leading editor was under some form of obligation, if not a firm commitment, to party-political backers."[156] Growth of mass circulation titles, like the *Daily Mail, Daily Mirror,* and *Daily Express,* at the turn of the century affected established newspapers like *The Times* which suffered steady declines of circulation forcing them to turn to wealthy benefactors, all with close links to government and the main parties, who recognised the influence newspapers had over an expanded electorate. Unionist support came from *The Standard* subsidised from Union Party funds; *The Globe* taken over by Burnhams Newspapers Ltd, a syndicate led by the wealthy businessman Dudley Docker in a deal arranged by Unionist Central Office; *The Observer* which received a £40,000 loan in 1914 from Central Office to fund the purchase of new equipment;

---

[156] George Boyce, 'The Fourth Estate: the reappraisal of a concept', in G Boyce, J Curran, P Wingate, eds, *Newspaper History - From the 17thC to the Present Day*, Constable and Company (London 1978) p29

and *The Pall Mall Gazette* that was purchased by Davidson Dalziel in 1915. Liberal support came from the *Daily News* purchased during the South African War by a syndicate organised by Lloyd George to advance the anti-war case and later taken over by George Cadbury; *The Daily Chronicle* sold in 1918 to Sir Henry Dalziel's pro Lloyd George syndicate; and *The Westminster Gazette* run by J A Spender with large donations from senior Liberal Party figures including Asquith and Grey.[157] The concentration of ownership shown below explains the narrow range of political comment that national newspapers provided. Lord Northcliffe controlled, in terms of circulation, over a quarter of the national market during the war with the *Times, Daily Mail,* and the *Evening News* having combined sales of 1.7 million daily copies. Northcliffe had close links with the Conservative party although he did not slavishly follow the Tory line.[158] He described his press as "Unionist and Imperialist" and, "supporting the unwritten alliance of English speaking peoples". His financial resources gave his papers a degree of independence from government that few newspapers possessed and his peerage was undoubtedly a means to retain his support.

---

[157] George Boyce, 'The Fourth Estate: the reappraisal of a concept', in G Boyce, J Curran, P Wingate, eds, *Newspaper History - From the 17thC to the Present Day,* Constable and Company (London 1978) p30
[158] J Lee Thompson, 'Fleet Street Colossus: The Rise and Fall of Northcliffe, 1896-1922' *Parliamentary History,* 2006, Vol. 25 Issue 1, pp117

Individual ownership and control over London papers 1914[159]

Lord Northcliffe		
(*The Times, Daily Mail, Evening News*)	1,700,000	28.9%
Daily News Ltd (*Daily News, Star*)	1,050,000	17.8%
Lord Rothermere (*Daily Mirror*) [160]	1,000,000	17.0%
Edward Hulton (*Daily Sketch*)	800,0001	7.0%
Frank Lloyd (*Daily Chronicle*)	400,000	6.8%
Syndicate (*Daily Express*)	300,000	5.0%
Davison Dalziel		
(*Standard, Evening Telegraph*)	260,000	4.4%
Lord Burnham (*Daily Telegraph*)	190,000	3.2%

London daily newspaper circulation in 1916[161]

Morning papers

Name	Political stance	Circulation[162]
Daily Chronicle	Liberal	400,000
Daily Express	Unionist	300,000
Daily Mail	Unionist	1,000,000
Daily Mirror	Independent	1,200,000
Daily News & Leader	Liberal	375,000 - 550,000
Daily Sketch	Independent	800,000
Daily Telegraph	Unionist	190,000 - 240,000
Daily World	Independent	
Financial News	Independent	
Financial Times	Independent	
Financial Truth	Independent	
Jewish Express	Independent	
Jewish Times	Independent	
Lloyds List	Independent	
Morning Advertiser	Independent	
Morning Post	Conservative	80,000
Standard	Conservative	80,000
Times	Independent	150,000

[159] John M McEwen, 'The National Press during the First Wold War: Ownership and Circulation' *Journal of Contemporary History*, 1982, Vol 17, pp471
[160] Lord Rothermere also owned the *Sunday Pictorial,* the *Leeds Mercury,* the *Glasgow Daily Record,* and the *Glasgow Evening News*
[161] *The Newspapers Press Directory*, C Mitchell Ltd (London 1916)
[162] John M McEwen, 'The National Press during the First World War: Ownership and Circulation' *Journal of Contemporary History*, 1982, Vol 17, p471

London daily newspaper circulation in 1916 (continued)

	Political stance	Circulation[163]
Evening Papers		
Evening News	Unionist	600,000
Evening Standard	Conservative	180,000
Globe	Conservative	20,000
Jewish Evening News	Independent	
Pall Mall Gazette	Unionist	10,000
Star	Liberal	500,000
Westminster Gazette	Liberal	20,000

Sunday Papers		
Illustrated Sunday Herald	Independent	
Lloyds Weekly News	Liberal	1,250,000
News of the World	non stated	1,500,000
Observer	Unionist	175,000
People	Unionist	550,000
Reynolds Weekly	Democrat	600,000
Sunday Pictorial	Independent	
Sunday Times	Independent	35,000
Weekly Dispatch	Unionist	500,000

Circulation Changes 1914-1918[164]

Year	*Times*	*Daily Mail*	*Daily Express*
1914	183,000	945,919	295,485
1915	1,105,214	372,840	-
1916	137,000	938,211	449,827
1917	131,000	973,343	578,832

[163] John M McEwen, 'The National Press during the First World War: Ownership and Circulation' *Journal of Contemporary History*, 1982, Vol 17, p471
[164] John M McEwen, 'The National Press during the First World War: Ownership and Circulation' *Journal of Contemporary History*, 1982, Vol 17, p482

BIOGRAPHY

Primary sources

Daily Mail
Daily Mirror
Daily News & Leader
Liverpool Echo
Lloyds Weekly News
Manchester Guardian
Observer
Times

Secondary sources

Paul Bew, *Ideology and the Irish Question 1912-1916*, Oxford University Press (1994)

Timothy Bowman, *Irish Regiments in the Great War – Discipline and Morale*, Manchester University Press (Manchester 2003)

D G Boyce, *Englishmen and Irish Troubles*, Jonathan Cape (London 1972)

G Boyce, J Curran, P Wingate, eds, *Newspaper History - From the 17thC to the Present Day*, Constable and Company (London 1978)

Gabriel Doherty and Dermot Keogh, eds, *1916 - The Long Revolution*, Mercier Press (Cork 2007)

Michael de Nie, *The Eternal Paddy: Irish Identity and the British Press, 1798–1882,* University of Wisconsin Press, (Madison 2004)

David Fitzpatrick, *The Two Irelands 1912-1939*, Oxford University Press (Oxford 1998)

David Fitzpatrick, *Politics and Irish Life 1913-1921 - Provincial Experience of War and Revolution*, Cork University Press (Cork 1977)

Michael Foy and Brian Barton, *The Easter Rising*, Sutton Publishing (Stroud 1999)

Tom Garvin, *The Evolution of Irish Nationalist Politics*, Gill and Macmillan (Dublin 1981)

Tom Garvin, *Nationalist Revolutionaries in Ireland, 1858-1928*, Oxford University Press (Oxford 1987)

Jonathan Githens-Mazer, *Myths and Memories of the Easter Rising*, Irish Academic Press (Dublin 2006)

Bill Hagerty, *Read all about it! 100 sensational years of the Daily Mirror*, First Stone Publishing, (Lydney, Gloucestershire 2003)

Peter Hart, *The IRA and Its Enemies*, Oxford University Press (Oxford 1998)

Peter Hart, *The IRA at War 1916-1923,* Oxford University Press (Oxford 2003)

Thomas Hennessey, *Dividing Ireland - World War 1 and Partition*, Routledge (London 1998)

Brian Inglis, *Roger Casement*, Hodder & Stoughton (London 1974)

Alvin Jackson, *Ireland, 1798-1998: Politics and War*, Blackwell (1999)

Keith Jeffery, *Ireland and the Great War*, Cambridge University Press (Cambridge 2000)

Keith Jeffery, *An Irish Empire? - Aspects of Ireland and the British Empire*, Manchester University Press (Manchester 1996)

Kevin Kenny (ed), *Ireland and the British Empire*, Oxford University Press (Oxford 2004)

Dermot Keogh, *Twentieth Century Ireland: Nation and State*, Gill and Macmillan (Dublin 1994)

J J Lee, *Ireland 1912-1985 Politics and Society*, Cambridge University Press (Cambridge 1989)

John M MacKenzie, *Propaganda and Empire - The Manipulation of British Public Opinion 1880-1960*, Manchester University Press (Manchester 1984)

Gary S Messinger, *British Propaganda and the State in the First World War*, Manchester University Press, (Manchester 1992)

H Montgomery Hyde, *Famous Trials, Roger Casement*, Penguin (Harmondsworth 1963)

Simon J Potter (Ed), *Newspapers and Empire in Ireland and Britain - Reporting the British Empire c1857-1921*, Four Courts Press (Dublin 2004)

Charles Townshend, *The British Campaign in Ireland 1891-1921*, Oxford University Press (London 1975)

Charles Townshend, *Political Violence in Ireland,* Clarendon Press (Oxford 1983)

Charles Townshend, *Easter 1916 – The Irish Rebellion,* Penguin Books (London 2006)

Michael Wheatley, *Nationalism and the Irish Party - Provincial Ireland 1910 - 1916*, Oxford University Press, (Oxford 2005)

Articles

Paul Bew, 'Moderate Nationalism and the Irish Revolution, 1916-1923', *The Historical Journal*, Vol 42 No 3 (Sep 1999) pp729-749, Cambridge University Press

Timothy Bowman, 'Composing Divisions: The Recruitment of Ulster and National Volunteers into the British Army in 1914', *Causeway Cultural Traditions Journal*, Spring 1995.

Timothy Bowman, 'The Irish at the Somme', *History Ireland*, 4, 4, 1996

Timothy Bowman, 'The Ulster Volunteer Force and the Formation of the 36th Ulster Division', *Irish Historical Studies*, 128, November 2001

David G Boyce, 'British Opinion, Ireland, and the War, 1916-1918' *The Historical Journal*, Vol 17, No 3 (Sep 1974) pp 575-593

John Campbell, 'Give a Dog a Bad Name' *History Today*, September 1984, pp14 -19

J. Curtice, 'Was it the Sun wot won it again? The influence of newspapers in the 1997 election campaign' *Centre for Research into Elections and Social Trends*, Working Paper Number 75, Sept 1999

Peter Hart, 'The Social Structure of the Irish Republican Army, 1916-1923', *The Historical Journal*, Vol 42 No 1 (Mar 1999) pp207-231, Cambridge University Press

Deian Hopkin, 'Domestic Censorship in the First World War', *Journal of Contemporary History*, Vol 5 No 4 (1970) pp151-169

John M McEwen, 'Northcliffe and Lloyd George at War, 1914-1918', *The Historical Journal*, Vol 24, No 3 (Sept 1981) pp651-672.

John M McEwen, 'The National Press during the First World War: Ownership and Circulation' *Journal of Contemporary History*, 1982, 17; 459

John M McEwen, 'The Liberal Party and the Irish Question during the First World War' *The Journal of British Studies*, Vol 12 No 1 (Nov 1972) pp109-131, The University of Chicago Press

Barry McGill, 'Asquith's Predicament, 1914-1918' *The Journal of Modern History*, Vol 39 No 3 (Sept 1967) pp283-303

John O Stubbs, 'Beaverbrook as Historian: "Politicians and the War, 1914-1916" Reconsidered', *Albion: A Quarterly Journal Concerned with British Studies*, Vol 14 No 3/4 (Autumn 1982 - Winter 1998) pp235-253

John O Stubbs, 'The Unionists and Ireland, 1914-18', *The Historical Journal*, Vol 33 No 4 (Dec 1990) pp867-893, Cambridge University Press

J Lee Thompson, 'Fleet Street Colossus: The Rise and Fall of Northcliffe, 1896-1922' *Parliamentary History*, 2006, Vol 25 Issue 1, pp115-138

Philip M Taylor, 'The Foreign Office and British Propaganda during the First World War', *The Historical Journal*, Vol. 23 No 4 (Dec, 1980) pp 875-898)

INDEX

Printed in Great Britain
by Amazon.co.uk, Ltd.,
Marston Gate.